DESTINY

Keys to Discovering and Fulfilling Your God-Given Purpose in Life

REV. WISDOM DAFEAMEKPOR

Contents

Endorsements

This book, *Destiny*, by Pastor Wisdom Dafeamekpor could not have come at a better time. We live in an age of teenage suicide, confusion and perplexity of mind at all levels of society. The big question is, "What has God said to you about where you are going in life?"

I recommend this book because, it throws fresh light on how to discover and fulfil your God-given purpose in life.

Archbishop Nicholas Duncan-Williams

The General Overseer, Action Chapel International

Destiny by Pastor Wisdom Dafeamekpor is a game-changer in a certain subtle way. It introduces several key factors critical to fulfilling our God-given purpose which are often overlooked. I have heard Pastor Wisdom teach over the years, now we have a book that establishes his deep understanding of divine truth. This book will take you into a new future!

Bishop James K. Saah

Chairman, college of bishops; Action Chapel International

Discovery surely provides momentum for *development* and places us into the arena of *deployment*. Destiny discovered, then, gives us a chance to sing destiny fulfilled and say with St Paul of a "fight well fought and a race well ran". The need for clarity then remains a focal point to equip each and every one of us in our pursuit of destiny.

Now comes the entry of a very fine Apostolic teacher with the commensurate pedigree to handle the issue of destiny. Rev. Wisdom Dafeamekpor who walks the talk, a man whose teaching ministry spans decades and still remains a fountain of sound teaching and depths of wisdom. His teaching ministry is so simple, yet very profound. Rev. Wisdom has a consistent, principled approach to ministry and an unwavering desire to hold aloft the Word through the years.

Today, he gives us the pleasure and blessing to sit at his feet with joy and receive biblical truths on DESTINY.

This book is surely an eye-opener that brings present truth so forcibly yet pleasurably home to us. It gingerly removes the scales of error from our eyes without damaging our interest for more truth and above all provides practical steps for the fulfilment of destiny.

This book comes with pace and punch, dispelling the myth and tearing up the evils of error served by secular humanism wrapped up in spiritual robes. A great addition to the Library of God, this book comes highly recommended and, truthfully I cannot hide my excitement at its entrance and my applause for the man I call a brother and a friend. This is surely a must-have and a must-read book for all.

Rev. Dr. Ebenezer Markwei

The President, Living Streams Ministries International, Ghana

As providence would have it, we are all purposefully dispatched on earth to carry out an assignment. Knowing it is one thing and accomplishing it is another. Carrying out both tasks can be equated with success. Rev. Wisdom Dafeamekpor seeks to help; both to discern and discharge your God-given mandate. Your life will be impacted and revolutionized. I have followed every page of this book and it has been revealing. It will do same to you as you embark on your journey of the rediscovery of your God-ordained destiny

Destiny has always been the plate of curiosity served on the table of life. I've seen the high and mighty, the low and weak, the rich and poor, and young and old trying real hard to unravel the tangled ropes of questions this topic brings.

The legitimacy of these questions can never be beyond debate, for the answers provided guiding lights for all to have an understanding of purpose and to seek the pathways and tools to accomplish purpose on the destiny road.

Bishop Tackie Yarboi

The General Overseer, Victory Bible Church International, Ghana

A wonderful contribution from the pen of an outstanding and eminent elder statesman of the Kingdom of God. The wisdom of God flows copiously from the pen of this hugely experienced man of God. For over four decades, Rev. Wisdom has stood as a giant in the pastoral and teaching offices in Ghana and beyond. This documentation of his acquired wisdom should be in everyone's library. Definitely a must-read book! I highly recommend this book to uplift you in your Christian life and journey. This book on "Destiny" is destined to be a major tool for the realization of all your visions and dreams.

The Lord bless you as you read.

Rev. Robert Ampiah-Kwofi

Global Revival Ministries, Ghana

Acknowledgements

I am grateful first and foremost to God Almighty for the opportunities He has given me to serve in His house, and learn of His assignment for my life. Through the lessons and experiences in His house, our eyes are opened to know that He has called us to live a life of destiny. We live to fulfil His purposes on earth.

I deeply appreciate the Grace Chapel Family for being my church family. Together we endeavour to discover and fulfil our God-given purpose in this life.

For the production of the book itself, I feel a deep sense of gratitude:

a) To My family –Lawrencia my wife and Joy my daughter for creating the space for me in the house to eventually write this book.

b) To all my friends who impressed upon me to go on this book project. In particular, I must mention Mr Edward Opoku and Deacon Bertrand Quaye of the Grace family for constantly reminding me to take time off and work on the book. Your pressure has finally paid off.

c) To my staff including Elikplim Banini and Mrs Sheila Addei for proof-reading the manuscript, and,

d)   To Tim Pettingale and my friend Olly Goldenberg for the immense work they have done in editing and proof-reading.

Dedication

I dedicate this book to a loving and selfless woman who is in her twilight zone and preparing for her final flight: Madam Beatrice Wosiegbe Dafeamekpor, my mother.

Mum, you have raised me up together with my six siblings single-handedly, with tough love, discipline and a mother's care.

I have watched your strong determination, toils and efforts to give us, your children, the best you can make in life, with a strong mother's love and instincts. These qualities left a deep impression on us.

Even though you are in your twilight zone, at the age of 103+ years, immobile in bed and in physical pain, we still savor our last moments with you as we discuss the contents of this book together and prepare for your final flight,

May your valedictory at the end of your destiny-journey mirror that of the Apostle Paul: 'I have fought the good fight, I have finished the race, I have kept the faith. Finally, there is laid up for me the crown of righteousness...'

Foreword

Many Christians struggle to know their destiny, often wandering aimlessly through life, pursuing the passions of this world, or repeatedly asking for prayer as they ponder their purpose.

As I read through this book, there were so many gems – not just for those seeking to know their destiny, but also for those who are actively pursuing it. The counsel of this book is not coming from a place of human experience or psychology, but from the Word of God. As such, the truths Pastor Wisdom discusses are both practical and applicable to all.

As you read this book, you will discover that God not only has a specific destiny for you to walk in, but you also have a responsibility to find that destiny. He has been preparing you for your destiny since you were created, even when you were unaware of it. Having discovered your destiny, you should then actively pursue it. Psalm 119 tells us that God's Word is a light to our feet and a lamp to our path. Through this book, God's Word is laid open for you to learn how to find and pursue your destiny. God doesn't want you to guess your calling, He wants to guide you into it. I believe this book will be a great tool to help you on your journey.

No comment on this book would be complete without a mention of the author. Reverend Wisdom Dafeamekpor is a remarkable man. When I first met him, almost a decade ago, I was struck by several characteristics: his humility, his love for the Lord, his love for the Word of God and his love for people. Jesus can be seen shining through him as he seeks to faithfully honour the Lord. Among other giftings, he is an excellent teacher who seeks to live out his messages in his own personal life. All of these characteristics, along with his decades of experience are poured into this book.

I count it a great honour that God has allowed our paths to cross and that I may count this man among my friends. He spurs me on to pursue my calling in the kingdom of God. May this book have the same impact on you as you pursue the destiny you were created to fulfil.

Olly Goldenberg

Children Can

Introduction

"But when it pleased God, **who separated me from my mother's womb and called me through His grace, to reveal His Son in me, that I might preach Him among the Gentiles,** *I did not immediately confer with flesh and blood, nor did I go up to Jerusalem to those who were apostles before me; but I went to Arabia, and returned again to Damascus."*
(Galatians 1:15)

By the time he wrote these words, the apostle Paul had realized that the call of God had been on his life since he was born. He looked back on the experiences and events of his life, seeing how far he had come in preaching the gospel of the Lord Jesus Christ and concluded that God had separated him *"from his mother's womb"*. This is the Bible way of saying "before he was born". Before he was born, Saul who became Paul, was chosen to preach the gospel of the Lord Jesus Christ. Paul's great realization is echoed in the word of the Lord that came to Jeremiah as a young man. God told Jeremiah, *"Before I formed you in the womb I knew you; before you were born I sanctified you; I ordained you a prophet to the nations"* (Jeremiah 1:5). Even before they were born, God had planned a life of purpose for these men, each with a specific assignment: to preach Christ and prophesy to nations.

Yet, look at the first part of Paul's life, before his conversion to Christianity on the way to Damascus. How did he spend his time? He consumed his energy by harassing and persecuting believers, putting Christians to death for professing that Jesus Christ was their Savior. He was busy destroying the very church of Jesus Christ that he was called to work for. Acts 8:3 puts it this way:

"As for Saul (Paul), **he made havoc of the church,** *entering every house, and dragging off men and women, committing them to prison."*

How could a man, called from his mother's womb by God to a life of preaching the gospel of Jesus Christ, spend the early part of his life causing havoc against the church? It was simply because he was ignorant of God's purpose for his life. He was unaware of God's destiny for him in this world. Hence, he was fighting against and destroying the very thing he should have been living for.

This truth teaches us a vital lesson:

If you do not know what your God-given destiny in life is, you may inadvertently spend your energy destroying what you should be building. You may be heading in the opposite direction, championing the wrong cause.

This is why it is crucial to discover early on, God's purpose for your life, so that you can fulfil your destiny. If you are diligent in this, you will accomplish your life's goals in good time and live a life of contentment and joy, instead of trials and errors. Many people are living life trying anything and everything that comes to hand, searching for purpose, later discovering this is not what they were made for. This leads to wasted years, wasted resources, regret, and ultimately emptiness. Many reading this book will recognize the wasted years in their own life. But all is not lost. Our God is a God of restoration, as well as the One who fashions the destiny of His people.

In Joel 2: 25 the Lord says to Israel, *"So, I will restore to you the years that the locusts have eaten."* Thankfully, our God is the One who can restore wasted years. With trust and faith in the God of restoration you can begin to discover His destiny for your life and begin an exciting journey to fulfill it. Like Paul, you can say much later in your life,

"I have fought the good fight, I have finished the race, I have kept the faith. Finally, there is laid up for me the crown of righteousness, which the Lord, the righteous Judge will give to me on that Day, and not to me only but also to all who have loved His appearing." (2 Timothy 4:7-8)

Join me now to explore and discover your God-given destiny as we study the life lessons of those in the faith who have gone ahead of us.

Pastor Wisdom Dafeamekpor

March 2019

1. Divine Encounters Lead to Destiny

"The heaven, even the heavens, are the Lord's; But the earth He has given to the children of men."
(Psalm 115:16)

When God created the human race, His plan was that we should have dominion over the earth. He gave the earth to the human race in order for us to establish His rule and kingdom on earth as it is in heaven. Due to Adam and Eve's disobedience to God, however, humanity lost their position of privilege and were consequently driven from the Garden of Eden. Nevertheless, God did not abandon man. Instead, He put into motion a plan to restore us to the glorious position of fellowship with Him that we enjoyed before, and to restore our mandate for dominion in the earth. Through His Son, Jesus Christ, we have now been redeemed and given the legal right to be restored to *son-ship*, glory and honor.

Ironically, it was God Himself who had to drive Adam and Eve from the garden when their nature became corrupted with sin, following their disobedience. The Lord placed an angel with a flaming sword at the entrance to the garden, to prevent them from returning. This stopped them from perpetuating their sin, and left an opening for their redemption. Even though God drove them from the place where they had enjoyed fellowship with Him, He had His own plan for their redemption. But this plan was not merely to restore fellowship with Him – it would give mankind a new nature; one which would not be under the dominion of sin and iniquity.

It was an elaborate plan which took thousands of years to fully manifest. It took years of preparing the human race to be ready to receive the Son of God amongst us – Jesus Christ, our Redeemer. Meanwhile, the human race began to take shape, outside of the Garden of Eden, with sin locked into the nature of man for the foreseeable future. Generation after generation were born in sin and grew up in sin, with a rebellious nature deeply embedded. Having lost precious fellowship and union with God, our lives could not match up to what God intended for us. Everyone fell short of the glory of God. No one, on his or her own, could make a meaningful impact in this world. No one could exercise dominion in the earth and live a fruitful life according to God's purposes.

Despite this limitation, as God prepared the earth for His redemption plan to unfold, He still appeared to various people at different times, and communed with His creation. Each of these encounters pointed towards His greater plan of redemption, which would enable men and women to live fruitful and meaningful lives. Through divine encounters, certain individuals became vessels through which the message of God's redemption plan impacted and benefited their generation.

Anyone who had an encounter with the Lord had his or her life turned in a God-ward direction and was left with a revelation of divine purpose; a calling and a destiny to fulfill. No one who encountered the Lord was ever the same again, apart from a few tragic cases where willfulness and disobedience derailed their life (such as Cain, who murdered his brother Abel). Most began living for a mission with a God-given purpose and impacted the generation in which they lived. They brought people closer to God, limited the impact of sin and rebellion on the earth, brought fruitful living into society, or played a special role in God's preparation of the earth to receive the Redeemer (before Jesus Christ came), or shared the redemption story with others (after Christ came). Their lives accomplished that which God had destined for them before they were born. They fulfilled their destiny and served their generation in the will of God.

This shows us how vital it is to have an encounter with the Lord God. Without God, our sinful nature compels us to wayward behavior, resulting in lost purpose in our life's endeavors. Our best intentions and efforts will spring only from self-serving ideas that, though they may seem good to us at the time, in the long run will be destructive. Any motivation generated from our sinful nature will just serve itself and not glorify God Almighty.

By contrast, an encounter with the Lord God leads us to discover the destiny He has for our lives. When we begin to follow that path of destiny, our lives become fruitful and a blessing to others. We make a positive impact on our world and bring God's redemption to others. In this way we fulfill God's purpose for our lives.

In the rest of this chapter we will look at the lives of three men – Saul, Moses and Gideon – each of whom had divine encounters with the Lord that transformed their lives in the following ways:

- They moved from meaningless pursuits to a life of distinct accomplishments.
- They moved from hopelessness, wandering in a desert, to a life of leadership and the pursuit of godly goals.
- They moved from fear, deprivation and defeat, to courage, hope and triumph over their enemies.

We will see how they discovered their God-given destiny in life, pursued it, and lived a life of accomplishment and restoration. They would all become vessels for God's redemption in their generation.

Learning from their lives, we may be encouraged to seek our own encounters with the Lord and transition from wanderings, unfruitful pursuits, hopelessness, fear, deprivation and defeat to lives in which we spend our days fulfilling our God-given destiny.

Saul's discovery of his destiny

At first glance, Saul's life doesn't look like a very good example for us to follow. God said of him, *"I greatly regret that I have set up Saul as king, for he has turned back from following Me, and has not performed My commandments."* However, we can learn useful lessons from him by examining how he was led to discover his destiny.

First, let's look at how he was described in 1 Samuel 9:1–3:

- His father was a Benjamite and a mighty man of power, influence and wealth.

- He was the most handsome man in Israel in his time.

- He was a man of great stature in Israel: *"From his shoulders upward he was taller than any of the people"* (v2).

- He was a desirable man, choice and goodly.

Saul started his life completely ignorant of what God had in store for him. Like a typical Jewish son, he was probably working for his father, tending to his herds and flocks of animals. He was born in a time when Israel was beginning to rise up against the prophet Samuel's leadership. They wanted to be ruled by a king, just like all the other nations around them, instead of by a prophet or priest .

Samuel was a great prophet of God. In Samuel 3:19, the Word of God says, *"And the Lord was with him and let none of his words fall to the ground."* Saul's servant described him in 1 Samuel 9:6 as, *"An honorable man, all that he says surely comes to pass."*

Yet Samuel did not do well in parenting his two sons. Just like Eli (the High Priest of Israel with whom Samuel grew up in the temple) Samuel failed to instill the fear of the Lord into his sons, Joel and Abijah, and seemed unable to discipline them . As a father, he desired that his sons would succeed him as judges, or priests in Israel, yet they fell into corruption.

"Now it came to pass, when Samuel was old he made his sons judges over Israel. ….. But his sons did not walk in his ways; they turned aside after dishonest gain, took bribes, and perverted justice." (1 Samuel 8:1)

The elders of Israel were angered by the induction of these two sons of Samuel. Undoubtedly, corruption should never be tolerated anywhere, let alone among the people of God, so it was perfectly justifiable that the elders stood up and spoke against the conduct of these boys. However, the elders of Israel went beyond simple anger against corrupt priests – they demanded that a king be appointed as ruler over them. They cited other nations as their example and rejected the priests in charge. But in the process, they rejected God as their King.

Don't most of us wish we were like someone else, even though God has made us all uniquely different? Sometimes the outward appearance of people's lives and their accomplishments can appear so attractive that we want to be just like them. We begin to desire what they have. Or we begin to act like them, even though we know nothing about what they are like inside.

By the time David Beckham was at the height of his success on the football field, my son, who was then eight years old, adored him. He loved both his football skills and his looks. One day, after teaching him about vision, I asked him what he would like to become when he grew up. His answer came in a split-second: "I want to be David Beckham when I grow up and captain the British national football team."

Sadly, I had to explain to him that captaining the British national football team and taking bending free kicks were hardly likely with our genes! However, it showed me once again that we can all desire or aspire to be someone or something that is outside of God's design for our lives. God did not intend for Israel to be led by a king at that time. But, seduced by the glamor of the kings of other nations, the elders of Israel decided they wanted a king to rule over them.

Samuel's failure as a father who did not train his sons to fear and serve God in holiness and righteousness, was surprising. Given his reputation as a prophet, you would imagine his house to have been a place where the Word of God was cherished and obeyed. Could it be that he was influenced by Eli's failure to discipline his own children? Consider the environment in which Samuel grew up.

In 1 Samuel 2:12 we read, "*Now the sons of Eli were corrupt, they did not know the Lord.*" While serving in the temple as priests they were in the habit of taking the sacrifices for themselves and defiling the women who came to work there. As a result, the Lord judged them, and they all died in one day.

Even though Samuel grew up in that environment, he was able to discipline himself and remained faithful to God, walking in righteousness and holiness. He never took bribes, nor defrauded anyone. He stood before the whole nation much later on in his life and challenged them regarding his integrity.

"I have walked before you from my childhood to this day. 'Here I am. Witness against me before the Lord and before His anointed: Whose ox have I taken, or whose donkey have I taken, or whom have I cheated? Whom have I oppressed, or from whose hand I have received any bribe with which to blind my eyes? I will restore it to you'. And they said 'You have not cheated us or oppressed us, nor have you taken anything from any man's hand.' Then he said to them 'The Lord is witness against you and His anointed is witness this day that you have not found anything in my hand.' And they answered 'He is witness.'" (1 Samuel 12:2–5)

Despite all of this, it was *his* children who provided the elders of Israel with grounds to demand the rule of a king, so that the military, judicial and religious leadership would be combined under one man. Amazingly, God agreed to their request and told Samuel that He would send a young man to him, who he should anoint as king over Israel.

Finding your stubborn donkeys

Against this backdrop, we come to the story of Saul and the lost donkeys. After grazing in the fields one day, some of Saul's father's donkeys never returned home. Kish asked his son, Saul, to look for the donkeys and bring them back. This should have been an easy job, to be completed in one afternoon, but Saul and his servant could not find the donkeys. They searched the fields and hills for three days straight and still could not hear the bleating of donkeys anywhere. A very frustrating experience!

Today, many people are searching for things in life that constantly elude them. Some chase after money day and night and never have enough. Some chase after pleasure, but their heart's desire is like a mirage. The more they search for these things, the further away they seem to be.

Saul's servant finally advised him that they should go to seek counsel from the man of God, Samuel. *"Perhaps he can show us the way that we should go"* (1 Samuel 9:6).

When you cannot find what your heart is searching for in life, instead of letting frustration drive you mad, one wise thing you can do is to go to the house of God and receive counsel. The Lord Jesus Christ has the answer to every problem, since He is the Creator and giver of life. He brought you into this world; He knows what your heart's desire is better than you know yourself. Go to Him and receive direction on the way you should go. Without His counsel or His Word operating in your life, you will be endlessly chasing after donkeys, going round in circles until frustration takes over your heart.

Encounter with the prophet

As Saul was approaching Samuel, the Lord confirmed to Samuel that this young man was the one to be appointed king over Israel. Without recognizing Samuel, Saul approached and asked for directions to the prophet's house. Samuel's response was very startling. He told Saul several amazing things:

- I am the seer (prophet)

- You will have lunch with me today in the high place

- Tomorrow I will tell you all that is in your heart

- What is in your heart is not the donkeys – the donkeys have been found

- All the desire of Israel (for a king) is on you and on your father's house

- You are the king that Israel is looking for

Saul was only concerned with finding his father's missing donkeys, but he received a "beyond-one's-wildest-dreams" prophecy. Furthermore, the prophet told him, "Tomorrow I will tell you what is in your heart." There were things placed by God in Saul's heart that Saul himself did not know or understand – probably because they were completely unimaginable.

"Eye hath not seen, neither hath ear heard nor hath it entered into the heart of man the things which God has prepared for those who love Him." (1 Corinthians 2:9)

Samuel was operating at this level because there had never been a king in the history of Israel before him. He responded as most people would when confronted with a special call from God. "I cannot do it; I am not qualified for it." Saul explained why he could not be king and his litany of reasons went like this (1 Samuel 9:21):

- I am a Benjamite

- The Benjamites are the smallest tribe in Israel

- My family is the least of all the families of the tribe of Benjamin

- Therefore, I cannot possibly be the king of Israel. Do not talk like that to me!

However, this was a divine encounter. Many events had occurred to bring Saul to this very place with Samuel and God would reveal what was already in his heart.

A vital conversation

"When they had come down from the high place into the city, Samuel spoke with Saul on the top of the house." (1 Samuel 9:25)

Samuel took Saul up to the roof of his house and they talked together for a long time, possibly into the early hours of the morning. Samuel shared with him both the prophetic Word from God and the knowledge of God: His will, His desires and His plans for His people, Israel. During this long conversation he probably told Saul what his heart really wanted in life and what God had made him for. Samuel likely told him about his leadership qualities and the passion in his heart.

Finding one's destiny in life has nothing to do with one's outward appearance. Saul was described as taller than anyone in Israel, charismatic and good looking. Everyone could see those outward qualities already – but it is the heart of a person that God sees and weighs. Therefore, we must conclude that the journey to discover our God-given destiny starts with discovering what goes on in our heart.

2. The Word of God Discerns the Heart

Samuel's sharing of the Word with Saul sets a pattern for us when we want to discover our God-given destiny. We have to spend time in the Word of God, the Bible. We cannot discover our true God-appointed destiny without the Word of God. When we bury ourselves in Scripture, the Word will reveal to us what God has placed in our hearts to fulfill. He speaks to us through His Word.

When Samuel told Saul, "I will tell you what is in your heart," he implied that Saul himself was not aware of what was in his heart. Similarly, there are God-given qualities hidden in you which you yourself may not be aware of.

The Word of God is able to discern the intents of your heart. It is able to separate what is in your soul from what is in your spirit.

"For the Word of God is living and powerful and sharper than any two-edged sword, piercing even to the division of soul and spirit, and of joints and marrow, and is a discerner of the thoughts and intents of the heart." (Hebrews 4:12)

Samuel's words to Saul revealed that there were qualities, desires and abilities deposited in the heart of Saul which would reveal his destiny as king over Israel. God would position him as king and those qualities would move him from the assignments of his biological father to a divine assignment – to fulfil the role of king, as desired by the elders of Israel. His God-given assignment in life was found in his heart, the center of his being, given to him by God. Even though he did not know it himself.

We may not meet a prophet like Samuel to tell us in such dramatic fashion what God has deposited in our spirits regarding our destiny. As we spend time in God's Word, His Spirit (who is always present when we are studying His Word) will continually show us, direct us, and reveal to us His destiny and our life's purpose. He will also give us desires, gifts, abilities, and grace which point towards and help us in these purposes. These may appear at various times in our lives through various circumstances.

Like Saul, we may currently be chasing donkeys. But, remember that chasing donkeys, being frustrated by not finding them, and the counsel of his servant, led Saul to the place of encounter with the Lord, which revealed God's purpose for his life. The truth is, God can and will use every experience in your life to contribute to you discovering His ultimate purpose for your life. Even your frustrations, wrong turns and mishaps can lead you to a place of seeking His face so much that you are drawn into discovering what He has planned for you. Take heart! When you are at a loss to know what your purpose on this planet is, that feeling of loss is a step in the right direction to discovering your destiny.

Spend time in the Word of God on a daily basis. You will be amazed how the quickening power of the Word will bring you to that place of knowing His purpose for your life. The Word will reveal what God has placed in your spirit.

Oil on the head of Saul

After Samuel had spent time with Saul and shared the Word of the Lord, the following day he anointed Saul with oil.

"Then Samuel took a flask of oil and poured it on his head and kissed him and said "Is it not because the Lord has anointed you commander over His inheritance?" (1 Samuel 10:1)

The act of anointing signifies a consecration; a setting apart for a sacred duty. Hitherto, only priests and the sanctuary or tabernacle had been anointed in the history of Israel. Saul was going to be the first king of Israel. By anointing him, Samuel was declaring that the position of a king was also sacred and important. It was not just a political position to be occupied on the basis of talent, skill or natural advantages.

The anointing brings out what is hidden in the heart of a person. It enhances and strengthens that which God has placed within. God's divine hand had to come upon Saul to energize him, strengthen him and empower him supernaturally to know, and to fulfill his destiny. Likewise, we too need the hand of God on our life. We need His anointing, His oil to be poured on our heads. Then we will be consecrated, set apart, energized and empowered to follow what He has placed in our hearts.

The remarkable thing about this anointing experience for Saul was that Samuel first anointed him in private. Before he was publicly proclaimed as king of Israel, there was a private encounter with the Lord. No one else was there. Later, in 1 Samuel 11, he went through the public process of being selected king of Israel by lot. The lot fell on Saul before the whole of Israel and he was proclaimed king.

The effect of the anointing in the pursuit of God's purpose

Before the public selection process, the workings and power of the anointing in private began to confirm to Saul that he was selected by God for a sacred duty – he was destined to be the king of Israel. Samuel told him that certain events that would occur on his way back to his father's house, would confirm to him that the impartation from the oil had begun to manifest:

- He would meet three men at Bethel who would give him two loaves of bread
- He would meet a group of prophets coming down from the high place with a stringed instrument, a tambourine, a flute, and a harp, and they would be prophesying

- On meeting them the Spirit of the Lord would come on Saul and Saul would also prophesy
- He, Saul would be transformed into another man

These signs came to pass exactly as Samuel said, giving Saul the confirmation he needed that the Word of the Lord he had heard from Samuel was indeed true.

The pouring of oil on his head was a physical act, which *symbolized* the Spirit coming upon him. But in the company of the prophets, the Spirit of the Lord *came upon him* and he began to prophesy.

The anointing of the Spirit on our lives lifts us into dimensions greater than our natural capabilities. The anointing is able to enhance the natural talents and gifts that the Lord has deposited in us. With the anointing on us, our natural talents and gifts can assume supernatural dimensions. In fact, 1 Samuel 10:9 says, *"So it was, when he had turned his back to go from Samuel, that God gave him another heart; and all those signs came to pass that day."*

Panicky heart or hiding humility?

When the occasion arrived for Samuel to announce to Israel that Saul was God's appointed king, Saul went into hiding (1 Samuel 10:17-23). He hid among the baggage of the Israelites. Samuel had called them to Mizpah for the king to be selected by lot. The casting of lots by the priest was one channel through which they would know the will of God under the Old Covenant. Today, once the Holy Spirit reveals to us what the will of God is, we can move ahead to fulfill what He is saying to us. There is no need to cast lots or seek other forms of confirmation (like Gideon's fleece, for instance).

The whole nation of Israel gathered at Mizpah waiting for Samuel to introduce them to their first king. At this time, only Samuel and Saul knew whom God had selected. The encounter Saul had with Samuel, the surprise announcement, the dinner at the high place, the discourse throughout the night, the anointing, the prophecies of the signs, the Spirit coming upon Saul, Saul's meeting with the company of prophets and prophesying, the change in his heart – all these should have prepared Saul for the big public announcement of his destiny as king of Israel.

But when the lot for the king fell on Saul, they looked for Saul among the crowd and could not find him! For a moment it appeared as if the lots had produced an imaginary person as king! When they enquired of the Lord, He answered them that Saul had gone into hiding.

"Therefore they inquired of the Lord further, 'Has the man come here yet?' And the Lord answered, 'There he is, hidden among the equipment.'" (1 Samuel 10:22)

Was it fear and panic or humility on the part of Saul? Why did he go into hiding instead of stepping out boldly to take his position as the first king of Israel? After all the preparation, assurances, mentoring and coaching from Samuel, it was surprising that he panicked on the big day and chose to hide. But it is not only Saul who behaves like this. How many of us have gone into hiding when the moment came for us to step into the open and lay hold of our destiny?

People hide behind excuses: work, children, family, or anything that can provide what appears to be a valid excuse. They avoid standing up at the critical moment when they are to be revealed to the public or step into the limelight. Perhaps it is fear, self-doubt, or just plain donkey-like stubbornness? Instead, we need to walk in true humility, which is the willingness to face the tasks the Lord has prepared for us to do as part of our destiny.

In spite of his initial display of fear and panic, Saul later exhibited two leadership qualities which Samuel might have been referring to when he said to him, "I will tell you what is in your heart." He showed a righteous anger against Jabesh Gilead and mobilized a fighting force that delivered Israel. He took the initiative and responsibility to lead the fight and obtained victory for Israel.

In 1 Samuel 11 a commander of the Ammonites, Nahash, came to lay siege against the Israelite city of Jabesh, located in the region of Gilead. The people of Jabesh Gilead became frightened and offered to become servants of the Ammonites in return for their safety. What more could Nahash have wanted? But Nahash declined the offer and gave them a condition before giving them a covenant. His condition was that the people of Jabesh Gilead should allow him to take out their right eye with a knife or fork first. After that, he would give them the covenant under which they would serve him. He wanted all the men in Jabesh Gilead to become one-eyed men!

Some people who allow the devil to use them behave this way. When they commence their acts of hatred against the people of God, they do not accept olive branches of peace. They are never satisfied until the people of God are totally disgraced. Trying to reason with them with arguments and logic does not work; only spiritual weapons in the heavenly realm can stop such people. Appeasement should be the last thing we consider giving to the devil and his agents.

When Saul saw the men of Gibeah weeping at their predicament he was puzzled and asked what it was that troubled the people? On being told the story of Nahash's threat, Saul's anger was greatly aroused. The Spirit of God came upon him and he was ready to do something about the situation.

It should no longer be a wonder for us to know that Samuel told him, "There is something in your heart; tomorrow I will tell you about it." There were hidden leadership qualities in Saul's heart. While others caved in and resorted to weeping, Saul rose up to confront injustice and seek the deliverance of the people. A true leader gets troubled at injustice and seeks to do something about it. Even if it is at the peril of his or her life, a person with a God-given destiny of leadership in his or her heart cannot tolerate oppression and will take steps to deal with it.

This is how some people find the pathway to fulfilling their God-given destiny. Does your heart get stirred up at the injustice in society?

Do you feel uncomfortable when you see helpless people weeping with hunger, disease, or from some other form of oppression? Maybe God has placed a passion in your heart for the helpless and voiceless groups in society? You may need to listen to your own heart to begin your journey of discovery.

Leaders take the initiative

Saul took the initiative and mobilized the men of Israel and Judah into a fighting force. He did not wait for Samuel to prompt him or spell out in detail what he should do. His heart stirred him up. He drew the motivation from a deep desire in his heart to stand against injustice and to deliver his people. Although he had been selected by lot and crowned as king, Saul had not assumed governmental authority yet. In fact, he went back to shepherding animals until his coronation in 1 Samuel 12! But Samuel had told him before in 1 Samuel 10:7, *"And let it be, when these signs come to you, that **you do as the occasion demands,** for God is with you."* So, he took the initiative and mobilized the men.

Leaders take initiative instead of waiting for someone to tell them what to do. Anyone who takes initiative easily will be stepping onto the dais of their destiny soon. Those who stay put and constantly wait to be told what to do will miss out. To discover your destiny in life, you must learn to take the initiative by drawing motivation from your heart's promptings and listening to the Spirit.

When Saul was mobilizing a force to fight Nahash, he sent a message out saying, *"Whoever does not go out with Saul and Samuel to battle, so it shall be done to his oxen."* Why did he mention Samuel's name when he had not talked with Samuel on this matter? Because he knew what Samuel would have wanted. People who step out with leadership qualities are quick to know and protect what their superiors would have wished if they were present.

In spite of his initial panic and hiding at the time of his public crowning, Saul began to show what was in his heart. Beneath his panicky heart and hiding humility lay the steel of leadership, which led to anger at injustice and an ability to take responsibility and initiative on behalf of the helpless. May this book help all its readers discover any God–given qualities that lie deep in the recesses of your heart!

Leaders take responsibility

Saul took responsibility for bringing deliverance to the people of Jabesh Gilead. He was ready to lead the people he mobilized to fight the Ammonites. In life, you will meet people who regularly complain at the problems in society, but have no desire to try and sort them out. But there are others who, in endeavoring to bring solutions to society, discover what their God-given destiny and calling in life are.

Saul did not procrastinate in this matter, wondering whether he should or he should not step out to help. The following day he grouped the volunteers into three companies and marched right into the camp of the Ammonites and went to battle against them. It was a one-day battle. He completely routed the Ammonites and put their survivors to flight.

Hesitation and procrastination prevent some people from discovering their God-given destiny. They receive the heart prompting, they get stirred up and wish there was a solution to the problem, but they either do not see themselves as responsible, or are never sure that they are carrying the solution themselves. They hesitate, procrastinate, and continue to murmur until the moment of destiny passes by.

In every discovery of God-given destiny there comes a critical moment of action – a moment when you have to step out and take hold of the opportunities presented. When your heart begins to stir, *step out and speak up.* In the moment of stepping out and speaking up, you may realize that you are easily accepted as the person chosen by God for this occasion.

That is what happened to Saul. When the people of Israel saw his leadership, how he mobilized and led the frightened and weeping men of Israel to defeat Nahash and his Ammonite army, they readily hailed him as their king. *"Then the people said to Samuel, "Who is he who said 'Shall Saul reign over us? Bring the men that we may put them to death."* (1 Samuel 11:13)

Some, probably because of Saul's panic and hiding on the day the lots fell, ridiculed him and wondered whether he could lead Israel as the king they desired. 1 Samuel 10:27 says, *"But some rebels said how can this man save us? So they despised him, and brought him no presents. But he held his peace."*

His brief panic made some rebels despise him, but the true leadership qualities and abilities which were in his heart were revealed when he rose to the moment and led Israel to defeat the Ammonites. Then, public acceptance was instantaneous. So much so that the extremists among them wanted those who had ridiculed him to be put death!

When you step out to do what God has deposited in your heart, you will be amazed at the acceptance and encouragement you receive.

"So all the people went to Gilgal, and there they made Saul king before the Lord in Gilgal … and all the men of Israel rejoiced greatly." (1 Samuel 11:15)

When you step out in faith, it will bring joy to others and great fulfillment and contentment to yourself.

Nahash – a provocateur for purpose

It is interesting to note that what Nahash succeeded in doing was to provoke Saul to act on what was in his heart. Saul was moved by stirrings from within himself. He acted as a commander and brought justice for the people of Israel. He would not hide behind excuses any longer. Nahash must be dealt with thoroughly and justice must be obtained for the people of Israel. This response contrasts with the response from the men of Jabesh-Gilead, which was fear, despair and weeping. Nahash provoked Saul to distinguish himself from the others.

Today, you may also have provocations around you. Provocations that stir you deeply and leave you disgusted with the problems you see around you. My prayer is that you search deep within your heart and see whether the Lord is stirring you to act. Has He already planted seeds that are nudging you to step out and speak up? Take time to pray and search your heart.

Summary of events leading to Saul's discovery of destiny

Let's recap on how Saul became aware of his God-given destiny. It is interesting to trace the series of events that led Saul to encounter the prophet Samuel, who gave him the Word of the Lord concerning his God-appointed destiny.

- The failure of Samuel to bring up his two sons properly in the fear of the Lord led to the elders of Israel petitioning for a king
- The missing donkeys of Kish. Saul's father sent his son Saul and his servant to look for the donkeys
- The donkeys were determined to play "hide and seek" for at least three days, leading to frustration on the part of Saul
- The advice of Saul's servant to Saul to go and consult the prophet Samuel

This led to the amazing encounter between the prophet Samuel and Saul. Through this encounter Samuel led Saul into discovering and accepting his God-given destiny, as the first king of Israel.

- The feast in the high place with Saul seated in a place of honor among the dignitaries and being given the choicest portion of the meat at the table
- The Word of the Lord to Saul, the counseling sessions, the anointing experience, the prophetic signs to confirm the Word of the Lord to him
- The day of castings lots publicly to select a king (which would be Saul by God's prior determination)
- Saul's panic moment and escape into hiding behind the equipment

Then a provocateur came along – Nahash the Ammonite. Saul rose to the occasion, reached down into his heart and showed great leadership qualities which included:

- Concern for the weeping of the men of Jabesh Gilead
- Courage and organizational ability in mobilizing 330,000 men into a fighting force
- Military strategy to defeat the Ammonites
- Magnanimity towards those who did not at first support his kingship

These qualities and longings were in his heart all along.

In discovering your destiny, the three great pointers you can consider today are:

a) Your life journey so far

b) An encounter with the living God

c) What is bubbling up in your heart

Your life journey so far might have been an uneventful one, yet through it all, the Lord has been preparing you to come to a place of discovery. The missing links in your life, the frustrations, near-misses, failures, searching for contentment and fulfillment, are all meant to drive you towards God. Against that background, an encounter with the Lord Himself, either directly or via His Word, the church, meetings with His servants placed in your way, and many divinely arranged coincidences will work together to bring you to the place of discovery. God's Word and His Spirit will be speaking to you constantly.

In the natural, Saul had great advantages, but they were not the critical factors that counted in his destiny. His height, looks, charisma, and parentage were enviable. In the natural one could say he was born with it. But as Samuel said to him, "Tomorrow I will tell you what is in your heart." As you read this book, may the Spirit of God stir your heart, so that you will know what He is calling you to. An encounter with God reveals what He has prepared you for. It reveals things in your heart that you may not be aware of. It leaves an indelible mark on your heart which cannot be taken away from you. The experience burns deep. It gives you a passion which you can draw from all your life.

These lessons were drawn from the early days of Saul. During his first two years, his story was a fantastic one. Samuel acted as his life coach, mentor and reference point. He was a king with a prophet over him. As long as he listened to Samuel, and paid heed to his word, he performed well as the king of Israel. However, it did not take more than two years for Saul to begin to show a stubbornness to the requirements of his position as king.

Knowing your destiny and fulfilling it are two separate matters. After two great years as king, pride and disobedience became Saul's hallmark. He disobeyed the instructions of Samuel and did whatever he pleased, instead of what would please God. He forgot the early days of his life when he went out looking for missing donkeys. He forgot that he did not even know what was in his own heart until the Lord, through Samuel, revealed it to him.

His first display of disobedience against Samuel's instructions was borne out of fear and impatience. Faced with an imminent battle against the Philistines, Saul decided to step into the priest's office and offer a burnt offering to the Lord. Instead of waiting for the prophet, who had the priestly duty to offer a sacrifice, he bowed to the pressure of the gathering of Philistines and offered the sacrifice himself.

According to the Law of Moses only priests were authorized to offer sacrifices to God. Saul's problems, his defiance of God, and disobedience to instructions of Samuel, his coach and mentor, led to a sad decline in his relationship with the Lord and he made a complete mess of fulfilling destiny.

May God enable us not only to discover our destiny, but to successfully fulfill it in true humility and obedience to Him.

3. Moses' Example of Listening to the Heart

Deacon Stephen in the New Testament was the first martyr of the Gospel of the Lord Jesus Christ. He was stoned to death by the Jews after they listened to his account of the Gospel. Before he was stoned (Acts 7), he recounted to the high priest and the onlookers the history of the deliverance of Israel from Egypt through the hands of Moses. In his recap, he gave some clues as to how Moses came to understand that he was destined to be the deliverer of Israel.

Moses was born at a time when Pharaoh decreed that all newly born Jewish males should be put to death. He did not want the Jewish population in Egypt to increase. But Moses' mother hid him for the first three months. After three months, he was taken to Pharaoh's house and his mother was hired as his nanny. His nanny (and mother) obviously influenced him and instilled in him who he was, regarding God's purpose for his life.

Moses' Childhood

During his childhood, Jochebed, Moses' mother would have gladly and excitedly told the little boy how his life had been preserved against all odds. He survived the satanic decree, through Pharaoh, that none of the newly born Hebrew male babies should live. The Egyptian midwives were instructed to put to death all male babies of the Israelites, but Moses survived. Then Pharaoh directed all the Egyptians to hunt out any Hebrew baby boys that had escaped and kill them. But Moses' mother's desire for her son to live was stronger than Pharaoh's decree of death. She prepared a basket and put him in it, placing him in the river at a spot close to where Pharaoh's daughter regularly came to bathe. She would have prayed and trusted the God of

Israel to deliver her son from danger and death. Miriam, his sister, was standing nearby on the river banks, hoping that Pharaoh's daughter would not destroy the baby boy Moses.

It must have been the hand of God guiding mother and daughter to fight and take risks for Moses' preservation. Pharaoh's daughter came to the river accompanied by her maids to bathe as usual. Her eyes caught the little basket with baby Moses in it. She knew this was one of the Hebrew children, but her compassion overruled her father's decree. She immediately decided to take the child and make him her son.

How could she nurse him? Miriam jumped from her standby position, appeared before Pharaoh's daughter and volunteered to find a suitable nurse who could take care of this adorable baby boy. Moses' mother was hired to nurse him. The plan worked perfectly. The risk that the mother took paid off. God's mighty hand was behind all these supposed coincidences to preserve the baby boy for his destiny.

Moses' mother would have told Moses that God had saved his life. The Lord preserved him from Pharaoh's satanic decrees and for three months her Egyptian neighbors could not find him. The Lord preserved him by preventing the crocodiles in the river from turning over the little ark she had made for him. She would have told him the favor of God prevented Pharaoh's daughter from turning him over to be killed. God had preserved his life *for a purpose*. There was a destiny for him to accomplish. While others died under the same decree, the Lord preserved his life.

As we also look back on our lives, we can recount many instances when the hand of the Lord preserved our lives. There are many dangers around us in this world, but until now our lives have been preserved. We have also been preserved for destiny. God has destiny for us to fulfill.

The mother did a good job of raising her little boy, instilling in him the truth that he was a Hebrew boy, destined to be a deliverer; not an Egyptian. She did this until Moses grew up and she had to leave

Pharaoh's daughter's house. By this time Moses' true identity and purpose in life were ingrained in his heart. Pharaoh's daughter took him and raised him from then on as her own son. *"And Moses was learned in all the wisdom of the Egyptians, and was mighty in words and deed"* (Acts 7:22).

It came into Moses' heart

In Acts 7: 21 we read, "Now when he was forty years old, **it came into his heart** to visit his brethren, the children of Israel. And seeing one of them suffer wrong, he defended and avenged him who was oppressed and struck down the Egyptian."

In spite of all the privileges he had enjoyed as Pharaoh's son for forty years, the things his mother had instilled in his heart from childhood stuck with him. It could not be removed by learning the ways and wisdom of Egypt. Stephen, recounting the history of Moses, said of him, "One day it came into his heart to visit his brethren, the children of Israel." His heart stirred him up. His heart began to speak to him. There was an awakening in him. What was in his heart concerning his destiny in life came to the fore and he remembered he was a Hebrew, so he wanted to see how his brethren were faring.

If you have godly parents and they make the effort to raise you in the fear of the Lord from your childhood, it can instill in you a sense of your destiny from God, right from your childhood. Moses' mother did a good job with him. The sense of his God-appointed destiny was embedded in his heart. His upbringing, and that which was in his heart, helped him to be keenly aware of his destiny as the deliverer of Israel.

In the field, when he saw a Hebrew man suffering wrong at the hands of an Egyptian, he so desperately wanted to deliver the man from his suffering that he killed the Egyptian. This was a bad start in fulfilling his calling. He depended on his own strength. He was hasty and did not have a coach or a mentor around, like Samuel, to guide him.

Moses' wrong timing and wrong strategy

Moses had the knowledge of his destiny, could not yield fully to the leading of the Spirit of God. There was no mentor around him. His mother, who would have guided him, had left Pharaoh's house long ago. Consequently, he slipped badly and ran ahead of God. This was not the moment to step out onto the dais of destiny. There were two and half million children of Israel in captivity and attempting to deliver them one by one was impossible. In God's plan the deliverance would come by mighty miracles, signs and wonders done through Moses' hands, but not by killing one Egyptian at a time.

Though he was destined to lead the Israelites out of Egypt, Moses needed to wait for God's timing and methods. After another forty years of chastening, shaping and transformation in exile, his moment of encounter with God's presence came in an experience with a "burning bush".

Moses' encounter with the consuming fire

Whilst in exile, Moses worked for Jethro as a shepherd and attended to his master's flock. While attending to his master's flock one day Moses had an unforgettable experience with a bush-fire. He saw flames of fire burning in a bush nearby, without the bush being consumed. In Deuteronomy 4:24, Moses told the Israelites, *"For the Lord your God is a consuming fire."* Yes, God Himself is a consuming fire. Ezekiel says in Ezekiel 1:27–28, *"Also from the appearance of His waist and upward I saw, as it were the color of amber with the appearance of fire all around within it; and from the appearance of His waist and downward I saw, as it were, the appearance of fire with brightness all around."* The presence of the Lord had come into the bush to speak with Moses. Right then, God spoke to him directly about his life's mission.

The Lord directed him to go back to Egypt and deliver His people – this was what has been in his heart all along. When he was a prince in Egypt in Pharaoh's court, he had wanted to see the children of Israel delivered from evil slavery. Now the Lord was sending him back to fulfill that destiny. Of course, he had been badly traumatized by the failure of his first, hasty attempt. It seemed like the desire to deliver his suffering brethren was now pushed into the deep recesses of his mind, buried by self-doubt.

Perhaps there are some people reading these pages who have buried their destinies due to failed attempts and self-doubts. It is almost impossible to revive a God-given desire on your own, so it was no wonder that God revealed Himself as fire to Moses during their encounter in the desert. As a consuming fire God is able to wake up such buried destinies in the heart of man. His fire brings back to life that which has died in the heart.

Divine encounter wakes up the buried destinies

The trauma Moses experienced from his failure and escape into exile was so deep that he objected to God sending him back to Egypt. Like Saul, he also tried to hide behind several excuses: I am not eloquent, I cannot do it, send someone else…

Let's take a look at his excuses.

- *Self-doubt:* he first tried to hide behind self-doubt. "Who am I that I should go to Pharaoh, and that I should bring the children out of Israel out of Egypt?" he asked God. Yet his mother had told him who he was and how his life was preserved for a divine purpose.
- *I do not know your name:* "Indeed, when I come to the children of Israel and say to them, 'The God of your fathers has sent me to you,' and they say to me What is His name?' what shall I say to them?"
- *They will not believe me:* "But suppose they will not believe or listen to my voice; suppose they say, 'The Lord has not appeared to you.'"

- *I am not eloquent:* "But I am slow of speech and slow of tongue." But in Acts 7:22 Stephen said Moses was learned in all the wisdom of the Egyptians, and he was mighty in words and deeds!
- *Send someone else:* "Oh my Lord, please, send by the hand of whomever else You may send."

It is difficult for those who have buried their God-given destiny to look beyond their failures and pick it up again. However, our God is the God of restoration and the God of second chances. Besides that, He is a consuming fire and manifests Himself in fire. His fire can warm you back into your destiny. If your destiny has been obscured by your past failures, He will patiently work with you and cause you to experience His fire until a glow comes upon your face again.

The supernatural encounter with the fiery presence of God turned Moses around and revived what had been in his heart since childhood – to be a deliverer of his people from bondage. The fire warmed his heart back to life and caused it to beat again with destiny.

Moses finally packed his bags and started his journey back to Egypt to fulfill his destiny. He intended to see the children of Israel delivered from the bondage of slavery and brought into freedom and liberty.

May the Spirit of God touch you today as you read this book. May He cause your heart to respond to His tugging and return to the moment when you gave up and let go of your destiny. Just because you are reading this book, it is not yet over for you.

4. Gideon's Encounter

Gideon grew up in an era when the nation was living in fear, subjected to intimidation from the Midianites (Judges 6). The Midianites had so overpowered Israel, plundering their crops and goods, that the nation was near starvation. The people had to hide and live in caves and strongholds in the mountainous areas. This went on for seven years and none of the Children of Israel could rise up and lead a battle against them. They were paralyzed by fear and intimidation.

But the Lord planned an encounter for Gideon that would change the situation for the nation. In the course of the encounter, Gideon was challenged by God to rise up and organize an army to fight the Midianites. The Lord sent an angel to meet Gideon at a time when he was secretly threshing wheat in a winepress. In his place of hiding an angel appeared before him and called him out, *"You mighty man of valor, the Lord is with you."*

The contradiction between the angel's greeting and his condition was so stark that Gideon let forth an angry response from his heart.

"If the Lord is with us why then has all this happened to us? And where are all His miracles which our fathers told us about, saying, 'Did not the Lord bring us up from Egypt? But now the Lord has forsaken us and delivered us into the hands of the Midianites.'"

The angel responded: *"Go in this might of yours, and you shall save Israel from the hand of the Midianites."*

We see here that Gideon believed in his heart that the Lord had forsaken them. He knew that if God had been with them, they would have easily defeated the Midianites. He knew that God is a God of miracles and that He delivered their forefathers from Egypt. The presence of the Lord with them would indeed have ensured victory, because no one can stand against God.

It was Jonathan, the son of Saul, who gave this revelation about the effect of the presence of God vividly to his servant. In 1 Samuel 14:6 we read, *"Come let us go over to the garrison of these uncircumcised; it may be that the Lord will work for us. For nothing restrains the Lord from saving by many or few."* Jonathan took his servant and the two of them, believing that the Lord was with them, attacked a whole garrison of the Philistine army. Their courage and faith stemmed from the revelation that they had the Lord's presence with them. They believed that God did not need a large army to defeat the Philistines. The critical factor was whether the Lord was with them or not – the presence of the Lord mattered.

Gideon, however, believed that the Lord had forsaken his people. And indeed He had! They had done evil in the sight of the Lord, and consequently the Lord took His hand of protection away from them and gave them over to the Midianites. The Midianites laid a siege around them and forced them into starvation. They needed a deliverer. Through this encounter with the angel, the Lord assured Gideon that He was with him and would deliver Israel through his hands. Indeed, his life's destiny was to be a deliverer of Israel in the time that the Midianites emerged as oppressors of Israel. But Gideon did not know God's purpose or destiny for his life. Instead of rising to the occasion, he succumbed to fear and intimidation. He was living in a cave and threshing wheat in a wine press, jumping at every shadow.

This is what ignorance of one's God-given destiny can do to a person. Ignorance can turn you into a coward and cause you to live below your dignity. Ignorance will make you live like others in your generation who accept oppression and defeat without a fight.

When Gideon had this encounter with the angel of the Lord, he came to believe that even though it might appear that the Lord had forsaken Israel, the Lord was in fact with him. In Judges 6:16 we read, *"And the Lord said to him, 'Surely, I will be with you, and you shall defeat the Midianites as one man.'"* He heard the sweet words of the Lord, "Surely, I will be with you." He already held the belief, just like

Jonathan, that if the Lord was with them, they would win any battle.

These words of assurance brought him the confidence he needed to step forward onto the dais of his destiny. He responded to them with an offering immediately. He prepared an offering with a young goat and unleavened bread. He laid them on the rock before the angel in reverence to the Lord. As the angel touched the offering with the end of his staff, fire rose from the rock and consumed his offering. The angel then departed and Gideon knew he was truly experiencing an encounter with the Lord God Himself. He knew that the Lord was with him and he could win the battle against the Midianites. He did not have to hide in a cave, living in fear, suffering starvation and misery at the hands of his enemies. This encounter helped him take on the boldness and courage of Jonathan. It made him come out of hiding and assume the mission of delivering Israel from his enemy.

Immediately after this encounter, Gideon began to take steps towards his destiny.

Today, the Word of God assures us in Hebrews 13:5 that God will not leave us. For us the born-again believer, under the New Covenant, in whatever circumstances we face, His Word to us is this: *"I will never leave you nor forsake you."* So, we may boldly say, *"The Lord is my helper; I will not fear. What can man do to me?"*

If your dream of God's purpose for your life is a big one, do not let the external circumstances of this life lead you to hide in a cave. Do not let fear of the obstacles in the way prevent you from stepping out to tackle what is in your heart; your God-given mission. Do not look at your present adverse circumstances and conclude that this is because God has forsaken you. The Word of the Lord says that He will never leave you nor forsake you. Do not feel forsaken by God because of the oppression of the Midianites of your day.

When you know in your heart that the Lord is with you, you can rise up and pursue the call of God on your life.

All along, Gideon's destiny in life was to be a deliverer of Israel! But Gideon was hiding in caves until this encounter with the angel of the

Lord. My prayer for every reader is that this book may also serve as an encounter – a meeting with the Lord through which you will come to the realization that there is might in your heart.

As the Lord told Gideon, *"Go in this thy might … have I not sent you?"* You may hear His voice in a whisper, or deep down in your heart, commissioning you to do things that will later lead you to His appointed destiny for your life. Remember He says to you, *"Surely, I will be with you, and you shall defeat the Midianites as one man."*

Through encounters, divinely arranged by God, all of these men changed. They began to see themselves differently and behave differently – as a prophet to the nations, a deliverer in Israel, and a king, the first king of Israel.

Interestingly too, almost every one of them who had this experience suddenly felt they were inadequate and began giving excuses, ranging from poor self-image to being too young. Yet, the word to Jeremiah summed it all up: *"Before I formed you in your mother's womb I knew you and ordained you a prophet to the nations."* (Jeremiah 1:5)

5. Seek Your Divine Encounter

Many people only discover their God-given destiny after they have had an encounter with His presence. Before that, they could not "hear" or understand the direction in which their hearts were leading them. This is not surprising, for many of us are so busy with our daily lives that we don't allow time to simply listen to our hearts or follow the stirrings of the Spirit.

On the other hand, there are also people whose hearts have been fixed on a course which the Lord has not planned for them. Their philosophy is to find the nearest available thing to do and get stuck in it for the rest of their lives. But they want to be someone that the Lord has not destined them to be.

In discovering our God-given destiny we need to receive instructions from the Lord Himself. He wants to guide us, to help us find the way He wants us to go. Just as the psalmist said in Psalm 32:8, "I will instruct you and teach you in the way you should go; I will guide you with My eye. Do not be like the horse or like the mule, which have no understanding, which must be harnessed with bit and bridle, Else they will not come near you."

Anyone desiring to discover his or her God-appointed destiny must seek an encounter with Him. We must be hungry and thirsty for His Presence and His special touch on our lives. Gideon was hungry and looking for the manifestation of God's days of glory and power. He remembered the stories of his forefathers, recounting the mighty deliverances of God by His outstretched arm and wondered where was the same God when Israel was suppressed?

It is your hunger that will drive you.

An encounter with His presence will reveal His purpose for your life and the destiny you should pursue. When you have an encounter with

Him, you will not travel on the same road you were on before. There is a power in His presence that transforms those who stand before Him and the more hard-hearted a person is, the more dramatic the encounter and transformation.

Not all with prophet, fire and angel

Peter was washing his empty net and musing about going home after a fruitless night of fishing when the Lord Jesus appeared before him. He asked Peter for his boat (Luke 5:1-11) and probed him on his efforts at fishing the previous night. Grudgingly, Peter followed His instruction to cast his net out one more time and miraculously brought in a boat-sinking catch of fish! Peter realized this was not natural and did not originate from human wisdom. He had come face to face with the Son of God and the presence of such a divine person was too much for him.

Jesus simply told him, "*Follow me and I will make you fishers of men.*" Peter's heartbeat was for fishing, but now Jesus said his fishing would be for men and women coming into the kingdom of God. A new destiny for Peter emerged out of this encounter with the Son of God.

Likewise, Zacchaeus (Luke 19:1-10) needed an encounter with Jesus. He was disadvantaged by being a very short man who could not see above waist height in a crowd. Not only that, his conduct in his tax–collecting business did not endear him to his fellow townsfolk either. Because of this, when the Lord Jesus passed through Jericho, no one would help him get to the front of the crowd and he had to climb a tree to get a glimpse of Jesus.

However, the Lord had in mind a divine encounter for Zacchaeus. Exactly when the Lord Jesus reached where Zacchaeus was at the top of the tree, Jesus stopped and called Zacchaeus to come down. The Lord went on to say that He would dine with him in his house that day! An encounter with the Lord Jesus Christ, the Son of God, in his own house was a delightful surprise to him.

Having come face to face with the Lord Jesus at the lunch table in his own house, Zacchaeus began to burst with new life. Without the Lord even preaching on the subject, transformation was taking place. His presence alone was working on the oppressive heart of Zacchaeus. Suddenly, Zacchaeus felt called to share half of his goods with the poor. From collecting taxes from the poorest people, on behalf of the Roman Empire, and at the same time quietly pocketing a substantial sum for himself, Zacchaeus now began a new mission. After his encounter with the Lord, he discovered that his true path and destiny was to help the poor and follow Jesus.

Out of these encounters with the Son of God, these men discovered their true destiny and purpose. Likewise, a divine encounter with the Living God will reveal our true destiny and mission in life.

God gives encounters to us in various ways. Some may be dramatic, and some may come gently, but every divine encounter will impact our hearts and release us into new or God–appointed destinies for our lives. These encounters either breathe new life into what He has already planted, or fashion our hearts into something completely new.

Some people will encounter His presence simply through His Word. Yet, this is still powerful enough to enable a person to discover his or her God–given destiny. Jeremiah puts it this way: *"The Word of the Lord came to me saying 'Before I formed you in the womb, I knew you; before you were born I sanctified you; I ordained you a prophet to the nations'"* (Jeremiah 1:4-5). Jeremiah was in no mood to take on a mission at his young age as prophet to the nations. But the Word of the Lord kept on coming to him and pounding in his heart until he began to fulfill that calling. But it didn't all go straightforwardly. At a certain time in the fulfillment of this calling, Jeremiah decided not to prophesy again. It posed too much of a problem for him. But the Word would not let him depart from that path. We read in Jeremiah 20:7-9:

*"Then I said, 'I will not make mention of Him, nor speak anymore in His name.' **But His word was in My heart like a burning fire shut up in my bones; I was weary of holding it back, And I could not."***

The effect of an encounter with the Lord on our destiny

A divine encounter will leave you with new purpose and release you into the journey of fulfilling your God-appointed destiny. The Lord was so gracious to appear to these men (Saul, Moses, Gideon, Peter and Zacchaeus) at a time when their journey was giving them little fruit. Their encounters with God changed them and their course in life forever. They received a new mission to accomplish. Their hearts began to beat with a new sense of purpose and destiny. In stepping out to accomplish their missions, they began a journey into their God-given destinies.

Moses gave up wanderings in the desert with Jethro's flock. He left behind his past failure in Egypt and its resulting sense of hopelessness. Now he could see himself again as an instrument of God's deliverance or a vessel through which the Lord would deliver Israel from captivity in Egypt. His heart was beating again with a new sense of destiny. We recall Stephen's earlier statement in Acts 7:23 that, *"It came into his heart to visit his brethren, the children of Israel."*

After Saul's encounter with the Lord he stopped the hopeless chasing of donkeys and began preparing for a new life as the king of Israel. Samuel had to teach him about royal protocol and how a king should behave and the boundaries that he had to observe (1 Samuel 10:25). Saul had new lessons to learn as his destiny lay before him.

Gideon's encounter with the angel of the Lord transformed him from a fearful "caveman" in hiding, to a bold, confident warrior who became willing to fight Israel's oppressive enemies. He could now see himself as a deliverer of Israel and an instrument to restore dignity and glory to God's own people.

Encounters with the presence and glory of God will transform your heart. This transformation will release in you a new sense of your destiny. It will birth in you a passion for the true calling in your life. It will become indelibly planted, deep down in your heart, as it did for these three men of God. Throughout the Bible many people encountered the Lord in this way, and they left with fresh passion in their heart for their calling.

Surely the Lord has also planned an encounter for you. Moments will come in your life when you will perceive that the Lord has His hand on you for a special purpose.

Out of those moments His presence will burn something so divine into your heart that you will not be able to shake it off. As He weaves His purpose and destiny deep within you, you will sense new passion and new direction bursting forth.

Finding destiny – my desire to help others

From my childhood days I have always had a desire to help people. While in school I concluded that I must study medicine and become a doctor, so that I could help people. I was certain that this was what God wanted me to do. He wanted me to help people, therefore I should become a doctor. In my teenage mind only doctors really helped people. I was already studying science in school, the only snag was the subject of Biology. I found the biology teacher very boring! She was an Indian lady whose accent was difficult to follow in class. To make matters worse, I just could not draw diagrams. I was never good at art and, to make matters worse, the biology teacher would always give diagrams as homework. Since I was always failing this Indian lady's tests in Biology, I erroneously concluded that I could not enter medical school. (I later found out that with good grades in Mathematics, Physics and Chemistry, I could still have entered Medical school, despite my poor drawings of animals and insects!). Instead, I settled on becoming an engineer.

Just before we completed the forms for our enrollment at University, I shared with a friend from another school that I was going to study mechanical engineering and become an engineer one day. He laughed so hard at the thought that I would be working with machines in a factory, putting on overalls with grease and dirt, and coming back home in my dirty overalls. Surprised by his reaction, I asked him what he was going to study? What did he want to become? He told me he wanted to study business management and become a manager in a big corporate organization. It is always interesting to listen to teens talk about how they are planning to spend their lives; what their goals are, their aspirations and hopes for the future. After our conversation, that picture of my friend as a well-dressed corporate manager stayed in my mind and, without much thought, I filled my enrollment forms out for business administration.

After I was born again at a Scripture Union Camp, my desire to have a career that directly helped people returned and became more intense in me. But here I was, about to enter University to study business administration and finance.

I recalled my childhood dream of becoming a doctor and became quite despondent. I had thrown away my opportunity to serve God as a doctor and now it was too late. I became very sad and confused. What should I do? I looked to Culain Morris, the then General Secretary of Scripture Union in Accra, to help me out. I needed his advice. If I'd messed up the one chance of doing what God had truly called me to do, would God have a Plan B?

Culain Morris was gentle and patient with me. He did not confirm a divine Plan B (which increased my agony). Instead, he first acknowledged that I had a God-given desire to help people, but patiently showed me that it did not have to be exclusively used through medicine. He counseled me extensively, seeing my anguish, and encouraged me to simply place my life in the hands of the Lord. He encouraged me to proceed to study business administration, but to trust the Lord to lead and use me as a vessel where and how He chose.

In the search for your God-given destiny, you must come to a place of total surrender in the hands of the Lord. When you are willing to live a life that fulfills His destiny, but are in a position where you do not know what that destiny is, you simply have to trust and rest in him.

We must be flexible and willing to go where He sends us. More than anything we are to yield to whatever way He wants to use us. We should become vessels in His hands, for Him to use in whatever way He sees fit.

His purpose may remain steadfast, but the method may vary according to our specific situation. As of now, I am not in the medical field, not in the corporate world, and neither in a factory with machines, but the opportunity to help people is all around. Even though it was not readily clear how my being in the corporate and finance world could help people, I placed my life in His hands. According to Culain Morris' counsel, God would lead me to fulfill His destiny no matter where I was.

I later realized that the invisible hand of God had always been working in me and through my circumstances over the years. After completing my studies at school, I found accommodation in a house which was also partly rented by an evangelistic association (HOVCEA) as its offices. I became friendly with the evangelist director of the group, Stephen Williams. He later took an appointment as the Pastor of Calvary Baptist Church. While I was dutifully working as a professional accountant, trying to build myself up in the financial world, he began to niggle me to assist him in the church on a part time basis. Initially, I was to help them set up proper accounting books and a good financial system for the church. I did not intend going beyond that as I was not a Baptist. He kept giving me more responsibility, including conducting teaching sessions, and, before long, I was fully immersed in church work as an assistant pastor! My desire for the things of the ministry began to grow to such an extent that it became clear to me that I was called to work as a minister and a teacher in the ministry of the Gospel of the Lord Jesus Christ.

Being in the ministry now, I am always inundated with people looking for help – spiritually, physically, or simply those who need someone to share the love of God with them. Now I am directly connected to a platform that gives help to vast numbers of people. I am in a position to offer help in many areas of life, not just ministering to the physical health of people. If that basic underlying desire to help people was a calling for destiny, then even though I made a detour into the world of corporate finance, my destiny was not over. Just like God did not conclude that Paul's destiny was over by his ignorant persecution of the Church, your destiny is not over. You can discover and fulfill what He has appointed you to do.

Culain Morris' counsel was wise: place yourself in the hands of the Lord entirely. As you proceed on your life's journey, be sensitive to His leading in the midst of detours and closed doors. He is so masterful that His invisible guiding hands will unfold the deepest desires He has planted in your heart at the right time. He did it for Moses, Gideon and Paul. He did it for me and He will do it for you too!

6. The Heart – Always the Vault of Destiny?

We have looked at the hearts of these men who discovered their destinies with the help of divine encounters. Some may ask, "So, will a modern-day prophet Samuel come to me and tell me in prophetic utterances what is in my heart, so that I know God's destiny for my life?"

Can anyone today just trust that what he desires in his heart will define the path of his or her destiny? Isn't it possible that our hearts can harbor self-seeking ambitions which we could misinterpret as God's destiny for our lives? These are valid questions.

History is full of stories of people who have attempted self-seeking, grandiose plans which they have conceived in their hearts, brooded over for a long time and decided to apply their energies and resources to achieve. Some have crashed miserably and drawn many people along with them into their disaster. One famous example in the Word of God is the generation which decided to build the tower of Babel. Genesis 11:4 says, *"Come, let us build ourselves a city, and a tower whose top is in the heavens; let us make a name for ourselves, lest we be scattered abroad over the face of the whole earth."*

Surely, this was a plan someone conceived in his heart and shared with others. To build a city was a great idea. To build a tower whose top would be in the heavens in those early days of man's history would have been a permanent wonder in the earth. It would have taken astonishing architectural and engineering skills. Even the pyramids of Egypt are still a tourist attraction and fetch the nation billions of dollars annually in revenue. The Eiffel Tower in Paris is a tourist attraction. At Kakum Park near Elmina, a wooden bridge hung in the tops of trees attracts many tourists throughout the year. The generation described in Genesis 11 was determined to build a tower that would reach the heavens. That would have been a landmark of enormous proportions. Some might have thought that the project would bring glory to God for giving man such wisdom and ingenuity, but the motivation behind their desire to build was not godly: *"Let us make a name for ourselves."*

What was in their hearts was not pleasing to God. Their sole purpose and motivation was to achieve fame among men. That could not be a destiny from God. God designs our destinies to bring blessing to other people, bring glory to His name, and make the world a better place according to His redemptive plan. He does not call us to build our fame before men or live for self-seeking interests. When left alone, the heart of the average person cannot dream of a life-destiny that will be a blessing to other people. Neither can the heart of the natural man design a destiny that glorifies God and fits within the eternal plan and purposes of God. Selfish ambition and self-seeking tendencies are part of the heart of natural man. They creep into all the plans conceived in the heart.

The heart is deceitful

When the Word of God refers to the heart of man, it is obvious it is not talking about the physical heart which pumps blood through our veins. It refers to our spiritual heart, the core and center of our being. Every human being on the planet is not only a physical person using five physical senses. There is an inner person – described as the heart – consisting of soul and spirit. We are all born with the "heart", the hidden man inside of us.

Prophet Jeremiah described this heart as deceitful and desperately wicked. Jeremiah 17:9 says, *"The heart is deceitful above all things, and desperately wicked; who can know it?"*

Thus, the heart can imagine vain things and consider them real. In fact, the Lord Jesus said, *"Out of the heart proceed evil thoughts, murders, adulteries, fornications, thefts, false witnesses and blasphemies. These are the things which defile a man"* (Matthew 15:19). If this is the natural state of the heart, how can it lead me to discover my destiny from God? Will it not deceive me and lead me to pursue projects or ideas of vain glory?

The promise of a brand new heart

The good news is that in God's redemptive process, He promises and gives us a new heart and a new spirit, which makes us new people for Him. Talking about this promise, Ezekiel prophesied to Israel and said to them in Ezekiel 36:26, speaking the words of the Lord, *"I will give you a new heart and put a new spirit within you; I will take the heart of stone (disobedient to God) out of your flesh and give you a heart of flesh; (that is, a heart which is responsive and obedient to God)."*

Those who have made Jesus Christ the Lord of their lives have received this new heart and new spirit at the time they surrendered to the Lord Jesus Christ. Those who decline to come under the lordship of Jesus Christ still possess their natural heart which the prophet Jeremiah described as "desperately wicked and deceptive".

The natural man has this desperately wicked and deceptive heart because of the disobedience of Adam and Eve in the Garden of Eden. The result of their disobedience is that the entire human race became dead spiritually, separated from the glory and presence of God. It is only by the redemptive work of the Lord Jesus Christ, His death on the cross, the shedding of His blood, and His burial and resurrection, that we can be born again and our spirits made new and alive to God.

There is a new birth experience described in the New Testament which the Lord Jesus established for us. The Lord told Nicodemus plainly, *"Do not marvel that I said to you, 'You must be born again.'"* The new birth takes place when you simply trust in Jesus Christ as your Savior and receive Him into your life as Lord. The Word of God reveals that His death on the cross was a sacrifice that He made for your redemption from the bondage of sin, death and Satan. Once you accept in your heart that His sacrifice on the cross was for you, you are forgiven and saved from the bondage and penalty of sin.

To be born-again

When the Lord Jesus died, He was buried in a grave. But He rose from the dead on the third day. By His resurrection, He showed that He has defeated the power of death, hell and Satan. He has become the Lord of all in the whole universe. When you call Him Lord and submit to Him, the devil has no legal authority any more to oppress you. The power of sin, in and over your life, is broken.

Romans 10:9-10 summarizes the new birth experience like this:

"That if you confess with your mouth the Lord Jesus and believe in your heart that God has raised Him from the dead, you will be saved. For with the heart one believes unto righteousness, and with the mouth confession is made unto salvation."

Believe in Him as your Savior and Lord, and the Spirit of God will begin His work of recreation in you right away. All that the Scriptures require from us is to believe in Him and call on Him for our salvation and His Spirit works in us right away to give us a new heart, a new spirit, and a new nature. This is why the Lord Jesus told Nicodemus, *"Except a man be born of water and the Spirit (of God) he cannot enter the kingdom of God."*

By confessing Jesus Christ, the Son of God, as our Lord, we receive this new heart and we become alive spiritually. His Holy Spirit fills our new spirit. We call this experience the new birth. In this, our new birth experience, we are created in God's righteousness and holiness. Our old sinful nature and old sinful ways are gone and there is now a new "you" whom the New Testament calls the New Man. We can trust that our new heart has new desires and longings which can eventually lead us to our God–appointed destinies.

Thank God that it does not require any additional work from us – just believe and call on Him. Paul said, *"For by grace you have been saved through faith and that not of yourselves; it is the gift of God, not of works, lest anyone should boast"* (Ephesians 2:9). God's grace has made available His salvation for us and, in this salvation process, we have a new heart and a new spirit.

As you read this book, I encourage you to believe in the Lord Jesus Christ. Know that His death on the cross was for the forgiveness of your sins and to win your salvation. Confess Him as your Lord, knowing that He rose from the dead. Call on His name today and invite Him to come into your heart as your Savior and Lord. As you do so, you will also receive your salvation and have a new heart and a new spirit from God today.

From now on in this book, whenever I mention "the heart" I will be referring to the new heart in the born-again believer. A heart that is renewed into righteousness and holiness by the Spirit of God.

"You will shiver"– my experience of being born again

Sunday evenings were our church service time when I was in Keta Secondary School. One day we had a guest speaker – a teacher from a school in the next town. This teacher was known for his strict discipline and extreme religious beliefs. We heard he was a bit weird in his ways. The services were compulsory so we had to attend. But this night we attended with added curiosity. We were eager to hear what this weird teacher had to say – and he did not disappoint. With his mannerisms and unique way of emphasizing points in the sermon, he kept us entertained. But his main point, and the one that I remember most vividly, was that he said, "If you met God, you would not be able to stand in His presence." He kept on saying, "You will shiver."

Truly, we found him strange. While he was preaching, we kept wondering how we could meet God in person. It didn't make sense to us. He claimed he had met God. We were laughing at him as he preached. He kept repeating, "When you meet God, you will shiver." We joined in with this refrain, "You will shiver," amidst our laughter. As the sermon progressed, our shouts got louder and his emphasis was getting stronger, as if we were in an argument. Before the sermon ended, we started to witness strange happenings. Some girls actually began to shiver. We couldn't believe what was taking place before our eyes. The man was preaching that we would shiver if we met God.

Right in the service, the shivering started.

Despite our astonishment, we concluded that it was just the girls in the junior classes being influenced to shiver by suggestion. However, while our mouths were still open in astonishment, we saw one of our classmates, Famous, sitting among us shivering and calling on God for His mercy. We were shocked. "Famous, what are you doing shivering?" we cried. His response was to call on God for mercy. So many questions flooded my mind: were my friends meeting with God? Had God's presence come into our service? I knew God was real, there was no question about that, but had He come into our midst?

Mercifully, the fiery preacher's sermon came to an end. The service ended and we dispersed, straightaway plunging into a discussion about what had happened in the service. Being students, the refrain "You will shiver" became the catch-phrase we used to tease those who had actually shivered. We said to everyone we perceived as religious, "You will shiver!" There was a Scripture Union group on the campus. We called out to most of them, "You will shiver." The weird preacher was a close friend of the patron of the Scripture Union. As for our classmate, Famous, we teased him so much that he later denied he ever called on God for mercy.

One Friday evening a group of us showed up at the Scripture Union meeting just for fun. That evening was like a set-up for another "You will shiver" night. This time it was the Scripture Union patron who began to act weirdly. He was testifying to the group that he had received the baptism of the Holy Spirit that day. At some point he began to speak in other tongues. I could not make any sense of this, except that I thought he was repeating what Jesus said on the cross: *"Eloi, Eloi lama sabachthani"* (Mark 15:34; "My God, My God, why have You forsaken Me?") I wondered why he was saying that? Had God forsaken him during the meeting?

Soon after that I became tense in the meeting; very tense. I started sweating as I sensed a presence in the room. I had the awesome realization that God was real and I was in His presence. I shivered, realizing that I was standing before God. I got up and told the Patron what was happening to me, glad that this didn't happen before the whole school! A deep sense of awe for God's presence was heavily on me.

The following day, early in the morning, I stole away (without asking for permission from the school authorities) to the beach to be alone to pray to God. I took a Bible along. After a few minutes of prayer, I ran out of words, so I started praying with the Psalms. I started at Psalm 1, reading the verses as my prayer, every word of every line.

By midday, I was satisfied that I had communed with God who had made me aware of His presence. This holy sense of reverence for God lasted a couple of days then gently evaporated from me. I could no longer feel that sense of reverence. The teasing or bullying of anyone religious was so strong in the school that it took a lot of courage to take a public stand and declare that you had become a Christian.

During the long vacation, the Scripture Union held its camp in the school. I enrolled with some friends just to kill time. The guest preacher from the next town – "You will shiver" – was there; the Patron of our School's Scripture Union group was there, alongside other guest camp leaders. In spite of their frightening presence, the camp was a lot of fun – singing, games, group discussions, prayer meetings and many other activities. It was during the morning Bible study in groups that everything came together for me. Some other leaders explained, in a way that I could understand, what it meant to be born again, to surrender your life to Christ and have a mission and a sense of purpose in life. In a sober moment of Bible study, the need to ask the Lord Jesus to come into my heart became apparent. Without hesitation, I committed my life to Him and believed Him for salvation.

I could look back on the "You will shiver" message, and my encounter with the presence of God in the Scripture Union meeting, as the Lord knocking on the door of my heart. When the Gospel was laid out plainly before me, step by step in the group Bible study, I readily invited the Lord Jesus into my life to be my Savior and Lord.

I have since enjoyed fellowship with Him. Every day I spend time reading His Word, praying to Him and listening to His voice. He is real to me and this fellowship with Him makes life worth living. Before you complete this book if you have not yet invited Him into your life, I encourage you to do so. You will be amazed to discover that He makes all the difference between frustration and fulfillment, between a defeated life and a victorious one, between living an aimless, routine life to having purpose, a destiny and a mission to fulfill on earth.

Jesus Christ, the Son of God, in your life as your Savior and your Lord, will lead you to discover and fulfill destiny.

Get set for the journey of discovery

To begin this journey of discovering your God-appointed destiny, you first need to be born again and receive a new heart. Through this, new desires and yearnings will spring up which are after God's righteousness, plans and purposes for our lives.

You can then begin to live your life from your heart outwards. The desires He has planted in you at the time of your new birth will grow and become your passion. Ignoring your heart and its desires can result in a very long, fruitless struggle.

If some of you are in a wilderness of discontentment right now, search your heart.

Proverbs 4: 23 says, *"Keep your heart with all diligence, for out of it spring the issues of life."*

If we are required to protect our hearts diligently because of the treasures that flow from it, then it follows that we are not to ignore the desires which are in our hearts. Do not ignore what interests your heart; do not ignore what causes your heart to rejoice; and do not ignore the desires or promptings of the Spirit of God in your new heart.

The Psalmist said in Psalm 37:3-5, *"Trust in the Lord, and do good; dwell in the land, and feed on His faithfulness. Delight yourself also in the Lord, and He shall give you the desires of your heart."*

Reading this verse, you may initially think that once you are dancing, jumping and twirling around in church, then whatever you fix your heart on as your desire will eventually be given to you. And, the more you rejoice in Him, the faster you will get it. On reflection, you will come to realize that your desires must first line up with His will for your life. A child of God should not desire things which are contrary to the Word of God and which are not in line with righteous living. Even seemingly harmless desires or wants which feed the flesh, may not necessarily be on the guaranteed list!

My heart's desires

What does the Word mean when it says that the Lord will give us the desires of our hearts?

As we delight in Him and seek to do His will, He will mold us and plant in our hearts the right longings and yearnings. Our hearts will only desire those things that are already in His plans and purposes for our lives. Our hearts will not be running after Satan's baits. We will not yearn to rob a bank, be corrupt, engage in prostitution, drug-trafficking, stealing from our employers, or anything that will bring shame and disgrace to the name of the Lord. Because our delight is continually in Him, He will embed in our hearts, in the deep innermost part of our beings, that which He has planned for us and is calling us to live for.

Thus, we do not determine on our own what our hearts' desires should be. He gives them to us. At present, they may be lying deep down in the innermost part of our hearts. But steadily, as we live our lives from the inside, we will be drawn to that which He has embedded in us. The desires He gives to us will begin to interest us. Some people recognize straightaway that what they are being drawn to resonates deeply in their heart. They begin to sense a passion for things that they were never really interested in before.

For other people, the recognition of what is in their heart will just be like a little flicker of light. As they pay attention to it, their interest develops and grows. It grows to the point where they are eventually consumed by it. Though it may require cultivation, once they begin to pay some attention to it, because it is a desire from the Lord Himself, He draws them into it. Even when it appears to be a chance discovery, something resonates with a chord in their heart. For the born-again believer who wants to discover the destiny God has designed for them, the desires in his or her new heart matter. But we will explore this later.

7. The New Man: Created for Good Works

"For we are His workmanship, created in Christ Jesus for good works which God prepared beforehand that we should walk in them."
(Ephesians 2:10)

In the previous chapter, we saw that the born–again believer is a new man or woman with a new heart and new desires. It follows that this same believer will have the opportunity to start a new life following God's prepared path or destiny for him or her. In fact, the Scriptures assert that God has already prepared a path of good works (Ephesians 2:10).

What has He prepared for us beforehand?

The *overall picture* of our destiny can be found in two verses of Scripture:

"Just as He chose us in Him before the foundation of the world, that we should be holy and without blame before Him in love, having predestined us to adoption as sons by Jesus Christ to Himself, according to the good pleasure of His will, to the praise of the glory of His grace, by which He made us accepted in the Beloved." (Ephesians 1:4–8)

"For whom He foreknew, He also predestined to be conformed to the image of His Son, that He might be the first born among many brethren." (Romans 8:29)

For all who believe in His redemptive work and saving grace, the Scriptures cannot make it any plainer. Amazingly, the Scriptures say that before the foundation of the world, He chose us for adoption as sons by Jesus Christ. Therefore, the overview of the destiny He has appointed for us is:

- To become and live as His sons and daughters through Jesus Christ
- That living as His sons and daughters, our lives will be to the praise of the glory of His grace
- That we will conform fully into the image of His Son, Jesus Christ

Our destiny in life starts with the decision to embrace fully our sonship – that is, to live daily as a son or daughter of the living God. There are people who have given their lives to the Lord Jesus Christ, but are not living their lives *wholly* as sons or daughters of God. How can this be? In our efforts to bring people into the new birth experience we stress the grace and faith aspect of our salvation experience. This is necessary. In Ephesians 2:8 we read, *"For by grace are you saved through faith, and that not of yourselves; it is the gift of God, not of works, lest anyone should boast."* Our works are not required for us to be saved or receive the new birth. What is required from us is simply to believe that Jesus Christ is our Savior and Lord. When we are born again, the Lord can begin to lead and guide us into the paths prepared beforehand for us to walk in.

Thereafter, we must live as sons and daughters of the Living God. We are no longer our old selves; we have a new life to live. Paul said it to the Galatian church this way: *"I have been crucified with Christ; it is no longer I who live, but Christ lives in me; and the life which I now live in the flesh I live by faith in the Son of God, who loved me and gave Himself for me."*

Discovering and fulfilling your destiny in this life will happen easily if you can also say that "Christ lives in me and the life which I now live in the flesh, I live by faith in the Son of God." You need to make a commitment to live daily by faith in the Son of God. It is daily living as a son of God, after you have been born again, that makes the difference between those who go on to fulfill their God-given destiny and those who don't. The Lord Jesus told the rich young ruler to, *"Go sell all you have, come take up your cross and follow me."* But this made the young ruler cry in anguish and despair. He had desired something from the Lord, but was not prepared to follow Him on a daily basis. Seeing the fulfillment of our destiny requires a daily relationship with Jesus Christ as a son or daughter of God.

Discovering Destiny as the believer with a new heart

You may not have had a burning bush experience like Moses; you may not have been struck by a bright light on a Damascus road like Saul; you may not have had a prophet like Samuel telling you what is in your heart; you may not have had an angel reveal to your parents the special assignments God has for you to fulfill in the world. But God still has a destiny for you to fulfill on the earth.

How then does a sincere believer go on to discover his or her destiny?

The first step – sonship

We have established, according to Ephesians 1:4, that God chose us before the foundation of the world and predestined us as His sons and daughters. So, our first calling is to "sonship". We are sons/daughters to the Father, like the Son of God.

In verses 5-6 we read, *"Having predestined us unto adoption as sons by Jesus Christ to Himself, according to the good pleasure of His will to the praise of the glory of His grace, by which He made us accepted in the Beloved."*

We are destined to be His sons and daughters. We do not have to struggle to be accepted by Him. We do not have to earn His acceptance. Once we surrender our lives to Jesus Christ the Son of God, and receive Him into our hearts as our Lord and Savior, we are adopted into God's family. We become His children by adoption. This is the first step in discovering our destiny and this is His will and good pleasure for us.

We are God's workmanship, made by the Master Creator of the universe, and like any father and child, He knows what is best for us and what will make us happy and fulfilled. Therefore, we need to press further into Him and discover the good works He has purposed for us.

Our next step – revealed by the Spirit

"But, as it is written: 'Eye has not seen, nor ear heard, nor have entered into the heart of man the things which God has prepared for those who love Him.' But God has revealed them to us through His Spirit. For the Spirit searches all things, yes, and the deep things of God.'" (1 Corinthians 2:9)

Under the New Covenant, the Spirit of God has been seeking (and is ready and willing) to reveal to us what God has prepared for us. Once we are "in Christ" and are sons/daughters of the Most High God, we are privileged to receive revelation from the Holy Spirit about our destiny. Instead of struggling to discern what could be His destiny or the prepared good works, we simply have to depend on the Holy Spirit to bring us into that knowledge and awareness.

Each person's destiny is unique. What God has prepared for you to fulfill in this life will not be a duplicate of what someone is doing in their life. As human beings we naturally look to others for inspiration or encouragement, but we must never think that by copying someone's actions we will have the same anointing or calling as them. We have to learn to follow the leading of the Spirit of God and keep our eyes solely on Him. He is the certain hope that our lives will be fruitful. Whichever way He leads us will eventually turn out to be the perfect destiny for us.

God has planned your destiny since before you were born. Since it is God who planned it for you, fulfilling your God-given destiny will be an exciting journey. Following God is not a boring venture. It is full of surprises and excitement as you see your hopes and goals come to fruition. When you discover your God-given destiny, be ready to be talked about. You may make news for ears to hear as you live out your destiny. As of now, your unique assignment may not have been talked about anywhere, but as you live out your life in pursuit of His destiny, soon "ears may hear" of it.

The plan which the Lord has for your life is undoubtedly bigger than anything you can imagine or dream of. You may have big plans and big dreams, but they are nowhere near as satisfying as those God has planned for you. So, how do we position ourselves to receive what He has in store for us? By intentionally leaning on the Holy Spirit, being close to Him and being in fellowship. Then we can learn, hear and receive everything we need to know.

The Spirit will lead you to discover and fulfill your destiny. He speaks to us; He draws us along certain paths. He knows the journey that we should take. Follow Him and run after Him.

If you want to have your destiny revealed to you by the Spirit, you need to fellowship with Him. This takes time. It is not a one-off event, but rather a lifelong relationship.

Being in a constant fellowship with the Holy Spirit should be part of our normal Christian life. 2 Corinthian 13:14 is a constant reminder to us: "The grace of our Lord Jesus Christ and the love of God and the communion (fellowship) of the Holy Spirit be with you all." Once we are maintaining the sweet communion of the Holy Spirit we can be certain that He will draw us after Himself into perfect paths for our lives. Indeed, He will draw us after Himself into the path of our destiny. Our duty is to follow Him, as He draws us. When you find joy in communing with the Spirit, discovering your destiny will come easily and without sweat.

Intimate fellowship brings divine revelation

In Genesis 18 we see Abraham enjoying a sweet time of fellowship with the Lord. He begged the Lord to prolong His visitation to him so that he, Abraham, would give the Lord some food.

"My Lord if I have now found favor in Your sight, do not pass on by Your servant. Please let a little water be brought and wash your feet, and rest yourselves under the tree. And I will bring a morsel of bread, that you may refresh your hearts. After that, you may by, inasmuch as you have come to your servant."

Abraham was glad to receive this visitation from the Lord. Now he wanted the visitation to be extended so that he could have time to minister to the Lord. His heart was yearning for fellowship and intimacy. Today, most of the time we are in a hurry to close our programmed services. Compare this with Abraham's attitude: he did not bring a catalogue of prayer points. His prayer was for the opportunity to simply minister to the Lord.

The Lord immediately answered, *"Do as you have said."*

Abraham joyfully jumped up to serve the Lord. He hurried into the tent to Sarah and said, *"Quickly, make ready three measures of fine meal; knead it and make cakes."* Then he himself hurried to the herd. *"And Abraham ran to the herd, took a tender and good calf, gave it to a young man, and he hastened to prepare it."* Contrast this with people who come to church late, people who can't be bothered to pray or read the Bible, and people who need coaxing to do anything for the Lord.

Abraham's act of preparing a meal was heartfelt worship. Pure, holy, and from–the–heart worship.

The Bible records many other times of sweet fellowship and intimacy between men and the Lord. After His resurrection, the Lord Jesus Christ met Peter and six other disciples and had a meal with them on the shores of the Sea of Tiberias. In this case, it was the Lord Jesus who cooked the meal for them, which is very interesting to think about, but the central point here is *fellowship*. In addition to the wonder and pleasure of being in the Lord's presence, what benefits does man derive from this fellowship with the Lord?

It was during his time of fellowship that the Lord gave Abraham a glorious promise: *"I will certainly return to you according to the time of life, and behold, Sarah your wife shall have a son."*

In an atmosphere of deep fellowship, the Lord often gives revelation to His people. It certainly would have been exhilarating for a 99-year old man to know that his wife was going to give birth in a year's time! But that was not the only thing the Lord was ready to reveal to Abraham.

As their fellowship continued, the Lord asked, *"Shall I hide from Abraham what I am doing …?"* We can deduce from this that the Lord does not hide His secrets, plans and future events from those who are committed to fellowship with Him. Do you want to know the destiny He has designed for you? Then let fellowship and intimacy with Him be your delight.

Maintain regular fellowship with the Lord. Be willing to give Him extended times of fellowship. It is like a meal to the Lord. Revelation flows in this atmosphere. He does not hide the future from His people. It was during an intense and extended time of worship (and serving the Lord His meal) that in Acts 13:1-2 the Spirit began to reveal to the church in Antioch that it was time for them to send forth Paul and Barnabas. For us to be led by the Spirit, we must be in continual fellowship with Him.

Knowing our God-given destiny is like travelling along a path. We may not have the full picture of what is at the end of the road, but we walk on His road in full assurance that where He takes us will be in the will of God.

1 Corinthian 2:11 says, *"For what man knows the things of a man except the spirit of the man which is in him? Even so no one knows the things of God except the Spirit of God."*

The Spirit of God knows what He has embedded in your heart. Through maintaining fellowship with Him, He begins to unfold, reveal and impart to you the passion that you need to walk in your destiny. Depend on Him and He will draw you along that path.

The desires of the new heart

"Delight yourself also in the Lord, and He shall give you the desires of your heart." (Psalm 37:4)

Let us look more closely at the desires of the new heart. The psalmist said, "The Lord shall give you the desires of your heart." When we first came to Christ, no doubt we rejoiced over this verse greatly. We used to take great comfort that, at long last, everything we wanted in life would be finally supplied. And we needed so many things: houses, new cars, good life-partners, high paying jobs, regular promotions, expensive clothes and much more. All that it would take was for us to "delight ourselves in the Lord" and the Lord would give us what we wanted.

As we grew older in the faith, however, we began to realize that it is the Lord Himself who plants His desires in us. He wants to give us what should be the desires of our heart – not the things we believe we need. He changes our heart so that our desires align with His desires for our lives. When His desires become the desires of our heart it is easy to discover our God-given destiny, because our hearts are full of all He has planned for us.

What is on your heart today? What are the godly desires that you hold there? Those things may be the very special works that He has fashioned and equipped you to do. Then you can say, "My part now is to pursue the Lord with great delight and follow the new desires of my heart."

But let us ask a serious question: if it is in our heart already, can we fail to discover it?

We may know someone who appeared to have great potential to affect their generation, but ended up making very little impact on anyone. We have heard the saying before, "I should have followed my heart." There are occasions when we come to a crossroads in our life. We are faced with a decision to make. We examine the situation and choose a direction. Some distance down the road we realize that we should have taken the other road; the road we are currently traveling is not leading us to the right destination. Often, people stop and look back, realizing that their hearts had forewarned them. They heard a voice within them, albeit faintly, telling them to take the other road, but they chose to ignore it.

When we make a decision, we often base it purely on logical facts. This is fine, except that as born-again believers, we are spiritual beings. Sometimes our minds may take one decision, but our hearts feel differently. We must listen to our hearts. On the occasions when I have looked back and said to myself, "I should have followed my heart,"

I have realized that the voice coming from within was indeed very faint. The mental analysis which led to my eventual logical conclusion, however, was very clear in my mind. I could hear my mind more clearly than my heart. Why couldn't I hear the decision in my heart more clearly?

In Luke 21:34, Jesus said, "But take heed to yourselves, lest your hearts be weighed down with carousing, drunkenness, and the cares of this life and that day come on you unexpectedly." The Lord Jesus teaches us that our hearts can become weighed down or sluggish. Carousing, drunkenness or even being anxious about the necessities of this life can make the spiritual heart dull, so that its voice becomes muted. If your heart is heavy with many concerns, its voice in you will be extra faint. It won't be able to get your attention when you are about to take a wrong turn.

What about the God-given desires of the heart? A wearied heart may not receive fresh revelations from God. It is too concerned about the cares of this life to be sensitive to the Spirit. A Christian could go through his/her entire life not realizing the destiny or good works that the Lord has fashioned for them.

There are many examples of people who had great desires, potential, talents and opportunities that could have enabled them to fulfill great destinies and impact generations, but they fizzled out, never realizing the "good works" the Lord had fashioned for them. This is spiritual "heart failure". The heart became weighed down with things of the world, things that did not truly matter, and the voice of the heart was drowned out.

What is the solution? If the God–given desires that lead to destiny are to be found in the heart, how do you keep your heart from being weighed down? The Lord Jesus says in verse 36, "Watch therefore and pray always that you may be counted to escape all these things that will come to pass …". In the next chapter we will look at this place of prayer.

8. The Place of Prayer

Prayer is a vital key to discovering your destiny. Even though we believe destiny is already planted in the heart of the believer, for the heart (inner man) to function optimally, the believer must be prayerful. Prayer keeps the heart from getting anxious with the cares of this life. Prayer takes the believer to God's throne room. From there, the believer can walk away free, having cast his or her burdens at the feet of the Lord.

Furthermore, in prayer we seek to know from the Lord what He has fashioned us for and what He has in store for us. In Hosea 6:3 the prophet said, *"Let us know, let us pursue the knowledge of the Lord."* We should know what God has destined for us, where He is leading us, and the talents and gifts He has blessed us with. The Apostle James put it this way: *"If any of you lacks wisdom, let him ask of God who gives to all liberally and without reproach, and it will be given to him"* (James 1:5).

We will turn our attention now to another well-known biblical character: Samson. He did not need to go on a journey to discover his destiny, because an angel of the Lord revealed it to his parents before he was born.

Manoah (Samson's father) and his wife had no children. One day an angel appeared to the woman and broke the news that she would become pregnant and give birth to Samson. The angel told her, *"Indeed you are barren and have borne no children, but you shall conceive and bear a son ... And no razor shall come upon his head, for the child shall be a Nazirite to God from the womb; and he shall begin to deliver Israel out of the hand of the Philistines"* (Judges 13:2-5).

Until now, Manoah's wife had been barren. I can imagine that this couple had prayed a lot for a child. They would have prayed for the barrenness to be broken and for the woman to become fruitful. They would have interceded for the Lord to turn their situation around. During their times of intercession, they would have remembered how Hannah had broken the curse of barrenness by promising her unborn child to the service of the Lord. Manoah and his wife would also have vowed their expected child to the service of the Lord. The Lord will take us up on such vows from a sincere heart. No doubt this couple's prayers were a factor that moved the hand of God to fashion Samson's destiny. In answering their prayers, the Lord graciously went further and revealed what He had destined the child for. He was to be a deliverer of Israel from the hands of the Philistines in his generation!

Prayer is one of the keys in revealing destinies. Prayer is a key that keeps the heart light and free to let the God-given desires already planted in our hearts spring forth.

We see a similar occurrence when an angel appeared to the priest, Zacharias (Luke 1:5-20), and told him, *"Do not be afraid, Zacharias, for your prayer is heard."* The angel talked about the birth of John the Baptist and what his assignment would be in life – a forerunner in ministry to the Lord Jesus Christ. Like Manoah and his wife, Zacharias and Elizabeth must also have had extended times of prayer to break the hold of barrenness on Elizabeth. They prayed throughout the early times of their marriage until they were old. They most probably left the matter in the hands of the Lord, resigning themselves to whatever the Lord had for them and continued to serve Him. But those prayers were not forgotten by the Lord.

Prayer is never in vain. The prayers of these men and women of God led to the revelation of the destinies of their children. It therefore is not surprising that when it comes to the state of our hearts, where destiny is conceived, the Lord Jesus Christ admonishes us strongly to always, *"Watch and pray."*

Burdens on the heart

Nehemiah was a man who discovered his destiny because of a burden on his heart. He was a cupbearer in the courts of King Artaxerxes of Persia. Cupbearers were required to select and serve wine to the king. They were required to taste the wine first to ensure that the king was not poisoned. Cupbearers also acted as informal advisors to the king. They were unofficial confidantes and, as a foreigner from Judah, it was a very good job to have.

Nehemiah's heart belonged in Judah, however, so when he met a man called Hanani who was visiting from there, Nehemiah asked about his people, the Jews, who had escaped captivity and remained in Jerusalem. He wanted to know how the city of Jerusalem faired. Hanani gave him some bad news. He was very frank: *"The survivors left in the province are there in distress and reproach."*

"What about the old city, Jerusalem?" Nehemiah asked.

Hanani said, *"The wall of Jerusalem is also broken down, and its gates are burned with fire."*

These words hit the heart of Nehemiah so hard that he sat down and wept. As he thought about the condition of his people and his beloved city, he became burdened for Jerusalem. The burden became so great that he was driven to do something about it. He first gave himself over to prayer and fasting and prayer, committing himself to this for many days, and asking the Lord to forgive all of the sins and iniquities that had caused the Lord to remove His hand of protection from them.

His prayer, recorded in Nehemiah 1:5-11, was passionate and heartfelt. However, he didn't just pray and fast, then leave it in God's hands. So strong was the burden that the following day, when the king saw him, the king exclaimed, *"Nehemiah, why is your face so sad?"* Then he perceived correctly and said, *"This is nothing but sorrow of heart."* In other words, the king told him that he was carrying a burden in his heart.

Nehemiah could not bear that his kinsfolk, the people of God, were in distress and living in reproach. He could not bear that the walls of

Jerusalem were broken down and the gates burned. Prayer was not enough. He felt responsible for helping to reverse this situation. He wanted to see the people of God free from distress, and the glory of Jerusalem restored.

This shows us that a person's destiny can be revealed by the burden the Lord places on their heart. This was Nehemiah's experience with the burden he carried for his people and the city of Jerusalem. Chapter 2:12 says, *"Then I arose in the night, I and a few men with me; I told no one what my God had put in my heart to do at Jerusalem…"* Through the burden on his heart, Nehemiah received from the Lord an assignment to restore Jerusalem – specifically to rebuild the walls of the city deliver his kinsfolk from reproach and distress. This led him to pursue and fulfill his destiny as a restorer and revivalist. He impacted his generation and left a legacy for the generations after him, simply by carrying out the burden he felt in his heart.

Do not ignore the stirrings of your heart. Do not ignore the burdens you feel in your heart for others. Do not ignore the burden you feel to bring change in deplorable situations. Those burdens, when you begin to act on them, may lead you on the path of your God-given destiny, like Nehemiah. Nehemiah 7:5 reiterates that he did not ignore the inclinations of his heart. He recognized them as coming from the Lord God. So, he said categorically, *"Then **my God put it into my heart** to gather the nobles, the rulers, and the people…"*

Nehemiah started with re-building the walls of Jerusalem. After restoring the walls he continued to follow the inclinations and stirrings of his heart. He fought to restore justice in Judah for the oppressed among them. When he learned that the rulers in Judah oppressed the poor and forced them into economic slavery, passionate Nehemiah rose up in anger. Moved by this passion, he challenged the rulers to return to the true values of freedom and liberty for the Covenant children of Jehovah. His passion was so great that the rulers agreed with him and said, *"We will restore it and will require nothing from them; we will do as you say."*

Nehemiah went even further and brought a great spiritual revival and a return to the Word of God through the public reading of the Law by the priest Ezra. The revival brought such repentance to the people of Judah that upon hearing the Word of God many were moved to tears. *"For all the people wept when they heard the words of the Law"* (Nehemiah 8:9).

Here was a cupbearer serving in a king's court. But destiny called out to him to bring restoration, repentance and revival to his people, the people of Judah. The call came through a burden placed on his heart.

Proverbs 4:23 says, *"Keep your heart with all diligence for out of it spring the issues of life."*

As you read this, I pray that the Lord will help you have an open heart to all He wants to give you. That every burden God places on your heart will bring you to the fulfillment of your great destiny!

Accelerating the discovery of your destiny

While some may take several years or decades to find out what their God-given assignment in life is, others discover it early and set about pursuing it with passion and zeal. This tells us that it is possible for one's journey to be accelerated or slowed down in life. Remember that the Israelite's journey to the Promised Land was just an eleven-day trip, but it took forty years to complete, and only two of the more than two million Israelites who left Egypt, made it.

There are factors that can accelerate the discovery and successful fulfillment of your destiny. These include maintaining a posture of delight in the Lord and associating with the right people. These two factors will help a believer to discover his or her destiny early on and to set them on a course of fulfillment.

Take Delight in the Lord
Psalm 37:4-5 says, "Delight yourself also in the Lord, and He shall give you the desires of your heart."

I grew up, and still live, in a part of the world that is characterized by poverty. During the eighties, Ghana experienced a famine and there was a severe shortage of food and basic necessities. Even a loaf of bread was difficult to find. Our response was to draw closer to God and pray for His intervention and help.

We prayed for help in our country, we prayed to survive, we prayed to have our daily bread and to break the chains of poverty and famine to receive abundance. Most of our prayer time was spent in supplication and intercession for our needs. I want to tell you that the Lord is always faithful to His Word. His promises are always, "Yes and Amen". In my lifetime we have seen the shackles of scarcity and severe lack largely lifted from our necks. There is a freer atmosphere in the country now. I am by no means claiming that poverty no longer exists but, thanks be to God, He has proved to us that He is a prayer-answering God.

However, the effect of growing up in such circumstances is that the prayer lives of the generation who lived through such hardship is mostly driven by need – the fight for survival; believing for the Lord's daily provision. We learned to follow the basic rules of prayer: start with *adoration*, move to *confession* of our sins, go onto *supplication* for our needs, and conclude by giving *glory to God*. But most of our prayer time was spent on the supplication segment. We grew up asking for our daily bread. Therefore, to spend time "delighting in the Lord" was not our usual practice.

But here is a direct command from the Word of God: *"Delight yourself in the Lord and He will give you the desires of your heart."*

It is ingrained in us that God is holy. Consequently, we usually approach Him with reverence and a holy fear. But in Psalm 37:4 the Psalmist says that we can also approach Him with a delightful glee – rejoicing in His presence. Surely, delighting ourselves in Him will involve rejoicing in His presence? How do we do that?

David is a great example of someone who expressed delight in God. Proverbs 37:4 says,

"Trust in the Lord, and do good; dwell in the land, and feed on His

faithfulness. Delight yourself also in the Lord, and He shall give you the desires of your heart."

David was someone who wasn't afraid to openly show his delight in the Lord. It is one thing to have passion in your heart – a controlled passion – and another thing to display that passion in an outward, spectacular manner. David showed his delight in God with unbridled passion and that is our challenge today as Christians: to show the world that we delight in the God who has saved us.

After David became king of Israel, the one thing he longed for was to restore the Ark of God to its rightful position in his kingdom. The Ark of God was the manifestation of the presence of God and He longed for the presence of God to be central in the kingdom. This is what he did.

"And David said to all the assembly of Israel, If it is of the Lord our God, let us send out to our brethren everywhere who are left in all the land of Israel, and with them to the priests and Levites who are in their cities and their common lands, that they may gather to us; and let us bring the ark of our God back to us, for we have not inquired at it since the days of Saul." (1 Chronicles 13:2-4)

He did not want to continue ruling without the Ark of God in its proper place in the kingdom. His concern was, *"for we have not inquired at it since the days of Saul."*

On their first attempt to bring the Ark back to the city, David organized a great procession of music to go before the Ark. 2 Samuel 6:5 says, *"Then David and all the house of Israel played music before the Lord on all kinds of instruments of fir wood, on harps, on stringed instruments of fir wood, on tambourines, on sistrums, and on cymbals."*

Such an organized music procession reveals David's deep joy and delight in the Lord. However, this first attempt ended in a disaster. Despite the new cart, the escorts, the ceremony and applause, someone breached the Lord's command. Uzzah, in his enthusiasm to stop the Ark from falling to the ground, touched it with his bare hands. This was unthinkable. It is us who need help from God, and not the other way around. In fact, Psalm 121:2 says: *"My help comes from the Lord, who made heaven and earth, He will not allow your foot to be moved. He who keeps you will not slumber; behold He who keeps Israel shall neither slumber nor sleep."*

Indeed, the Lord's presence in the Ark was not asleep and did not need the help of Uzzah to avoid falling. Because he touched the Ark, Uzzah died on the spot.

The fear of the Lord

This shows us that alongside delighting in the Lord, it is important that we also revere and fear Him. We read in 2 Samuel 6:9 that, *"David was afraid of the Lord that day ..."*. Often, being in awe of the *holiness* of God leads us to do the right thing.

Similarly, Paul writes in 2 Corinthians 5:11, *"Knowing therefore the terror of the Lord, we persuade men (to receive salvation as we must all appear before the judgment seat of Christ)."*

Delighting in the Lord and expressing that delight does not exclude the fear of the Lord. David showed that he also feared the Lord when he said that he could not handle the Ark of God. He directed that the Ark of God be sent to the house of Obed-edom the Gittite to keep. Poor Obed-edom! How would he manage to keep the Ark of the Lord in his house without further disasters?

Presumably, David was also asking that same question himself. No wonder the prophet Hosea 6:3 said, *"Let us know, let us pursue the knowledge of the Lord."* Puzzling the king all the more was a report in town that after three months of hosting the Ark of God, the Lord was blessing Obed-edom and everyone in his household. Obed-edom was just performing his duty as a host to the Ark of God, but his blessings were supernatural and could be attributed only to the presence of the Ark of the Lord. The very thing which brought disaster to Uzzah, brought supernatural blessings to another person.

Proverbs 25:2 says, *"It is the glory of God to conceal a matter, but the glory of kings is to search out a matter."*

David decided to go back and bring the Ark of God from the house of Obed-edom to the city of David. If Obed-edom's house was blessed, then the whole city of David must be blessed. Listen to what David himself said to the Levites this time:

"You are the heads of the fathers' houses of the Levites; sanctify yourselves, you and your brethren, that you may bring up the ark of the Lord God of Israel, to the place I have prepared for it. For you did not do it the first time, the Lord our God broke out against us because we did not consult him about the proper order. So, the priests and the Levites sanctified themselves to bring up the ark of the Lord God of Israel. And the children of the Levites bore the ark of God on their shoulders, by its poles, as Moses had commanded according to the word of the Lord." (1 Chronicles 15:12-15)

David, after seeking out the correct way to move the Ark, managed to bring it safely to the city of David. Later he confessed that, on the first attempt, he had not consulted the Lord. The ark was to be borne on the shoulders of the priests, not driven by mules or donkeys pulling a cart. Even though the cart had been brand new with soft cushions, the Lord had wanted His presence to be carried on the shoulders of His priests.

Now that the Ark was back in the city, David could not hide his joy. He truly delighted in the Lord.

Every six paces they took, David ordered a sacrifice of oxen and fatted sheep (2 Samuel 6:13). David himself danced with all his might before the procession. He knew he was dancing before the Lord, delighting in Him. He leapt, jumped and whirled before the Lord, throwing off his kingly robes and making a public spectacle of himself.

When you delight in something precious you cannot hide it. Real delight cannot be hidden. A true delight in the Lord will show in our expressions. Our quest to know Him more and more, our longing for His presence, and the desire to be guided by Him, should all flow from our taking delight in Him. Delighting in Him also means that we hold Him in reverence and awe. David's delight was not *replaced* with fear when Uzzah died. The fear of the Lord came alongside the delight. Both attitudes can exist in one's heart at the same time. In fact, to possess the fear of the Lord and wish to do things His way is a result of our delight in Him.

Delighting in the Lord does not mean just a smile on our face. David's dancing, leaping in the air, whirling around, and de-robing so that he could dance with all his might even though he was the king, all go to show what the psalmist meant when he said, *"Delight yourself in the Lord and He will give you the desires of your heart."* Delight involves the expression of our emotions as well – joy, gladness, and excitement in the presence of the Lord.

Can the excitement be too much? Most of us today, if we saw David's type of dancing in church, would not classify that as delighting in the Lord! In 2017 I was at the *Heaven Come* conference hosted by Bethel Church in California. I was completely blown away by the worship and the presence that the worship released. One of the ladies leading the worship sang *What a powerful Name it is*. In 2018, on the first Sunday during another visit, I went straight to a church where I thought she was leading worship, expecting to experience the same heavenly singing. I was wrong. She was not there. The church that I mistakenly had gone to consisted of mostly youth. Not surprisingly, it was a very noisy church service meeting in a night club. However, everything was great! Talk about expressing their delight! I was going to dash straight out and say, "This is not for me" but had to remind myself that Psalm 100:1 says, *"Make a joyful noise unto the Lord."* It does not say "a controlled noise". It is a noise that *must* be made because you are bursting with joy and excitement.

Take note of David's answer to his wife, Michal's criticism of his behavior. David answered her, *"It was before the Lord … Therefore, I will play music before the Lord. And I will even be more undignified than this and will be humble in my own sight."*

Part of humility is that you put your kingly robe aside and express your delight in the Lord your God.

Like David, when you long for the presence of God, you will be willing to pay any price to be there. When you possess the fear of the Lord alongside your excitement, and can take His chastisements and be corrected in your ways, when you are willing to express your heartfelt delight in Him, surely God will reward you out of His pleasure.

The psalmist said, *"He will give you the desires of your heart."* Your destiny will be revealed to you through the desires He plants in your heart.

Associating with the right people

We all have a destiny planted in our hearts which is unique to how the Lord has made us, but there is another important factor. Being with people who are similarly focused on fulfilling their destiny means that their faith and enthusiasm rubs off on us. It can ignite in us a similar desire to find out what His will is for us.

For instance, I have noticed that most second generation leaders discover their destiny by getting alongside their first generation leaders. The charisma of the first generation pulled something out of them.

In Proverbs 13:20 we learn that, *"He who walks with wise men will be wise; but the companion of fools will be destroyed."*

When Elijah passed by Elisha and threw his mantle on him (1 Kings 19:19), Elisha immediately recognized that he must associate with Elijah if anything significant was to come out of this symbolic spiritual act. Truly, what God told Elijah was, *"Go and anoint Elisha as prophet in your place."* The Lord had already decided that Elisha should replace Elijah in the prophetic ministry. Somehow, Elisha knew that he could not jump from being a farmer to becoming a prophet on his own. He must associate with Elijah.

There had to be a process through which he would discover clearly what God had in store for him. Once the mantle touched Elisha, even though Elijah continued to move away from him, Elisha ran after Elijah. He followed Elijah from then on, served him and was with him until his time on earth was fulfilled. Elisha stuck so closely to Elijah that when Elijah tried to send him away at the time of his transition to heaven, he could not convince Elisha to leave him alone. Elisha stuck with Elijah right to the end of his life's journey and saw him depart into heaven in a chariot of fire. He could point out the place where the horses of fire landed.

That level of deep association with a man, so focused on his God-given mission in life, would spark fresh fires of discovery in anyone. There is great power in associating with the right people. When you see them fulfilling their God-given destiny, you will also be urged on to become aware of your destiny; to seek to know what the Lord has in store for you.

The twelve disciples, whom the Lord Jesus called to be with Him, had the greatest privilege of associating with the most influential man on earth. It wasn't the teaching that had the most transformative impact on them, it was simply being close to Jesus; being in His presence.

The way John put the association in his epistle is this:

"That which was from the beginning, which we have heard, which we have seen with our eyes, which we have looked upon, and our hands have handled, concerning the Word of life – the life was manifested, and we have seen, and bear witness, and declare to you that eternal life which was with the Father and was manifested to us." (1 John 1:1-2)

John was talking primarily about the effect their *association* with the Lord Jesus Christ had on them.

In the process of that close association, they heard Him speak, they saw Him act, their hands touched Him and, as a result, they could bear witness and declare Him and His eternal life to others. The close association with Him transformed them so that they could find their own purpose and destiny, knowing that they were chosen to be witnesses and announcers of eternal life. Their association with Him was not just for fun – it led them to know their destiny in life.

In fact, in Matthew 19:28 the Lord Jesus said to them, *"Assuredly, I say to you, that in the regeneration, when the Son of Man sits on the throne of His glory, you who have followed Me will also sit on twelve thrones, judging the twelve tribes of Israel."*

Jesus revealed what God had planned for them, not only in this life but in the life to come. Because He is God in the flesh and knew all things, in both this life and the hereafter, He could tell them about their destiny.

When you associate with people who are fulfilling their destiny, their attitude and purpose rubs off on you. It sparks the search within you to know what you are here for.

Paul took young Timothy under his wing and tutored him, not in a classroom setting but in the crucible of ministry. As young Timothy travelled with Paul, served him and watched him in the fires of ministry, something was burned in Timothy as well. Because of his association with Paul, Timothy became an overseer or Bishop over the churches planted in the Crete region. He found out his destiny and fulfilled it. Through his letters to him, Paul urged him on in life and ministry and taught him to impact not only the generation in which he lived, but also the generation which would come after his allotted time on earth. *"You therefore, my son, be strong in the grace that is in Christ Jesus. And the things that you have heard from me among many witnesses, commit these to faithful men who will be able to teach others also"* (2 Timothy 2:2).

Paul urged him to prepare and impact the next generation by committing to faithful and able men the training, the truths, and the way of life he had given to him. In fulfilling one's destiny, our eyes should also be on impacting the generation that is to come after us. His association with Paul prepared Timothy well to discover and fulfill his own God-given destiny.

My lesson about association

I remember an incident in my school days which taught me vividly that the associations we make in life will affect its outcome. Though it was a national holiday, the school authorities had announced that all students should attend class and do private studies. There would be no break for us! That morning the boarding house seemed like a prison to me. I was not in the mood for studying during a holiday. What I really wanted to do was to go home and visit my mother (about four miles from the school) and enjoy a home-cooked meal – something I'd not had in a long while. However, with no exeats from the school, the only means of seeing my mum for a meal was to break the school rules and sneak out unnoticed through a gap in the fence.I recalled on our last Speech Day, that the guest speaker, a military man, had spoken to the school about discipline. He gave a good speech and exhorted us to be good students, obedient during our time at school. He then amazed everyone by concluding with what he called his "golden rule", which was: "When you have to, break the law, but don't get caught and you will still be a good student"! There was uproar from students and teachers alike and everyone laughed. Of course, the main thing we students took away from this was, "Don't get caught!"

Armed with this "leeway", I made my way to the fence at the rear of the property, removed the temporary wooden panels, and slipped through. The school's security men dutifully guarded the main gate and only periodically patrolled the back, so I felt safe. It turned out I was not the only one with this brilliant idea! That day around ten of us sneaked out successfully. All of us were sixth form students with A level examinations to sit in a few week's time.

We set off and chatted excitedly about not being caught. Initially, we seemed to be going in the same direction. "Where are you going?" I quizzed the other boys. To my surprise they were heading for the Palm Wine Bar, which was located along the way to my house. A wine bar – so early in the morning? It became clear to me that there were the "gangsters" of the school, notorious for breaking the rules. My plan was to enjoy a good home-cooked meal, but theirs was simply to get drunk.

Well, all of us ended up in the Palm Wine Bar. I reasoned, "Never mind, I'll just spend 30 minutes with them, since we are all chatting and laughing." I told myself I would only have a drink of the fresh, same-day tapped palm wine (which to me was a refreshing drink) and avoid the strong fermented alcoholic palm wine. We ordered the two types of wine in pots. Some of the boys did not come from our area, they were from the cities Accra and Tema, and not used to palm wine. They duly become so intoxicated that they moved outside and began dancing in the street. Oncoming vehicles swerved to avoid hitting them. They took things a step further and began acting like traffic wardens, flagging down vehicles.

Of course, this was terrible, but the rest of us were laughing and enjoying the scene, watching our colleagues harass innocent drivers. Looking back, it is puzzling how it never dawned on us that news of such a public display of arrogance and bad behavior would make its way back to the school authorities, just a couple of miles away. Proverbs 20:1 is correct when it says, "Wine is a mocker and beer a brawler; whoever is led astray by them is not wise" (NLT).

The next vehicle to come along the road was the school bus, carrying the boarding house master and assistant headmaster. Once again the unruly boys jumped into the middle of the road. Seconds later they recognized the vehicle and its passengers. The furious school masters got out of the bus and ordered them: "Get inside!" Those of us still sitting under the palm trees realized the game was over. It wasn't funny anymore! We were all taken back to school in the bus with our tails between our legs.

Shortly after, the news of the misconduct of eleven students who went on a drinking spree and took over the main road broke throughout the school. Most of the student population were angry about the damage done to the reputation of the school in the community. The biggest surprise to many, however, was my inclusion among the gang of eleven student-drunkards.

Throughout my stay in the school I had always been well-behaved. It was difficult to explain that I was actually going for a home-cooked meal, and that I had only drunk the non-fermented, same-day tapped palm wine.

The real effect of my association with the drinking-group of students that day, brief as it was, came when we faced the school disciplinary committee of housemasters. The discipline was swift and severe. They had had enough of students getting drunk and misbehaving. We were suspended from school for six weeks. This meant we would go home and return only to take our A level examinations. It was obvious this was going to have a telling effect on our A level results, with the possibility that our admission into university might be affected. The results of this association was going to have a bearing on two year's study of sixth form and I would not be able to attend the final six weeks of classes before the exams, which included teacher review sessions and group studies.

I quickly learnt the lesson of associating with the wrong crowd. I felt the crushing weight of the guilt. Added to this woe, how would I explain to my widowed mother what had happened? It taught me that those you associate with will affect your future in one way or another. It is much better, therefore, to choose who we will associate with in an intentional manner. It's not good enough to drift into associations by coincidence or chance. Even if circumstances push us together with certain people, we can still review those associations and decide whether they will have a positive or negative effect on our destiny. Associations must be based on the values we cherish. Wine is a mocker!

As soon as I compromised my values and chose to associate with intoxicated friends, disaster struck. Watch your associations – they will affect your destiny!

Today, think about who you associate with. Search out men and women of destiny who know where they are going in life and have the same hunger and passion to serve the Lord.

The power of right associations on one's destiny is vividly exemplified by the story of Ruth, a Moabite girl and Naomi. Ruth was a Moabite girl who, under normal circumstances, should not have had any inheritance in the history of the Jews. However, she chose to settle in Bethlehem with Naomi, her mother-in-law. There was no reason for her to accompany Naomi back to Bethlehem, except that her soul clung to Naomi with affection and adoring service.

Naomi was her mother-in-law but Ruth's husband (Mahlon or Chilion) died. Naomi herself had also lost her husband, Elimelech. She then decided to return to Judah, her home country, after learning that the economic conditions had improved in Judah. She was returning as a widow who had lost her husband and her only two sons in the land of Moab. Thus, she was coming back home destitute, with very little material possessions, but a lot of sorrow and pain in her heart for the wasted years she spent in the land of Moab. There was nothing attractive about Naomi except that she was a Jewish woman.

The two daughters-in-law, Ruth and Orpah, decided to go along with her in search of new fortunes in her home country. On the way, Naomi thanked and blessed them for their faithfulness to her and her children. She advised and urged them to stay behind and live among their own people, the Moabites. She prayed for them to find new husbands and a new life. Orpah eventually heeded her advice, kissed her goodbye and left.

Ruth, on the other hand, drawing from some instincts deep in her heart, refused to leave Naomi. No amount of explanation and urging by Naomi would convince her. She finally poured her heart out in these words:

"Entreat me not to leave you, or to turn back from following after you; For wherever you go, I will go; And wherever you lodge, I will lodge; Your people shall be my people, and your God, my God. Where you die, I will die. And there will I be buried. The Lord do so to me and more also, If anything but death parts you and me." (Ruth 1:16-17)

Eventually, the two of them returned to Bethlehem. Together, they tried to make a new life; to discover what to do to have daily bread. In the process, Ruth began a journey, under the coaching of Naomi, which led her into contact with one of the most eligible bachelors in Bethlehem, Boaz. Naomi herself got excited at the prospect of a potential relationship.

Firstly, Boaz was a relative of her late husband and, by extension, entitled to inherit the widows in the house. Secondly, Boaz treated Ruth favorably and sought to protect her right from their first meeting in the field. Thirdly, Boaz was not married, even though he was prosperous, and he probably would have been looking for a suitable lady to take as his wife.

Naomi, being the experienced Jewish woman, guided Ruth skillfully to position herself for a journey that would define her destiny and her place in history. Under the guidance of Naomi, and by Boaz' own invitation, Ruth frequented Boaz' farms to glean and obtain their daily provision of crops. The skillful Naomi set up the discussion about marriage with Boaz, who had already become enamored with Ruth. Boaz took Ruth as his wife.

The wonder of this episode is that Boaz was a very influential man in Judah. Boaz and Ruth gave birth to Obed who brought forth Jesse the father of David. These great men were in the lineage of the Lord Jesus Christ, the Son of God. Ruth was a Moabite woman. Earlier, God had forbidden the Jews from mixing with the Moabites as they were said to be a cursed race. How could a Moabite woman find her way into the powerful lineage that the Lord Jesus Christ came from?

Ruth's association with Naomi was a destiny-defining association. When you associate with the right people, your life can be lifted up and placed on new paths which you could never have dreamed of. The right association with the right people can change your course and help you discover your God-appointed destiny.

My own response to the call of God into ministry was accelerated by my association with other ministers who are on the cutting edge and exercising impactful ministry. I have enjoyed a good relationship with some outstanding ministers in our country. Their zeal and total commitment to the Lord, which I witnessed at close quarters, created a "burning fire" and a passion within me. This passion and zeal enabled me to change course and enter the full time ministry of the Gospel of our Lord Jesus Christ. Prior to my deepening relationship with ministers, I was content doing part-time ministry over the weekends in a lively Baptist church. In the midst of such strong, impactful ministers I was continually challenged to listen to God's voice within me and respond to what I perceived to be the higher call from the Lord.

Consequently, I transitioned from the finance world into ministry without looking back. Association with the right people who are fulfilling their destiny will influence you to seek and discover your own God-given destiny. You will be swept by the currents of that association onto your own path of destiny.

Seven Attitudes required to fulfill your God–given Destiny

Our main goal in life, as believers with new hearts and new spirits, should be to live as sons and daughters and to discover what God has created us to do. But discovering His destiny for us on its own is not enough. We must *fulfill* our destiny. This requires a lifetime's commitment and obedience to His leading through His Word and Spirit.

For this life-journey, we need to cultivate certain qualities in our character. Fulfilling destiny is not a course that can be taught in school. These character-qualities are developed in the crucible of real life. Without these qualities, you could have multiple divine encounters with fire, angels, prophets, visions and dreams, or have your destiny clearly written on the wall, and still end up living a mediocre life that makes no impact on anyone. The Apostle Peter wrote to the Jewish believers, *"Who have obtained like precious faith with us by the righteousness of our God and Savior Jesus Christ,"* reminding them that they needed to add to their faith certain qualities in order to live meaningful and fruitful lives.

For the believer today to live a life that fulfills his/her special assignment from God in the earth, seven attitudes or character traits must be formed: courage and boldness, desire and hunger, diligence, humility and persistence. We are going to explore these in the chapters that follow.

9. Courage and Boldness

The Courage Factor

Everyone will need courage at some point in their life. Some people define courage as facing their fears. Chills may be running down your spine, but you still keep going forwards because deep down you know that you have a mission to accomplish. This determination best describes what we call *courage*.

If we want to follow our God-given destiny for our lives, we will soon realize that what the Lord is calling us to is bigger than our capabilities. Our God-given destiny will always stretch our faith and leave us feeling inadequate. This feeling of inadequacy can cause us to fear and doubt whether we have what it takes to accomplish our destiny. For some, a lack of resources to finance their dreams can cause them to refuse to even start their mission. In other cases, they may be so aware of the power of the enemy that they become crippled with fear. They are unable to do anything because they are paralyzed. To press through this fear we need the spiritual force of *courage*. Courage comes from knowing God intimately. It is prophesied in Daniel 11:32 that, *"They that know their God shall be strong and they shall do exploits."* Inner strength comes from knowing that God releases courage in us to tackle what He has called us to do.

Finding Courage

One of the monuments in Ghana that serves as a tourist attraction is the Kakum forest. There is a walkway constructed with ropes on top of the tallest trees. Visitors are encouraged to take the walk and get a good panoramic view of the forest and the surrounding villages and towns.

I took a British family of six, who were on holiday, for a visit there. We were given the rules: you walk in a line; no two persons walk abreast; once you start you must finish the journey; you are not allowed to return halfway because of the people behind you.

The starting place of the walkway was at ground level, but you walk your way up. It all looked fun and entirely safe. We began to walk and ascended higher and higher. Of course, we were holding onto the side ropes for balance and safety. The four kids with us were enjoying the walk and giggling. At some point, us four adults stopped talking, and I noticed that some were swaying slightly on the walkway. It was still safe, but there was this gently swaying motion. I looked down and noticed that, by now, we were way up in the air, level with the tops of some trees.

At that point, I realized I didn't like this experience. There and then I decided that I shouldn't risk my life with this. I had believed the forest officials on the ground when they assured us of our safety. There were also people ahead of us who were marching on quite comfortably. But I was not happy with the swaying. We were way up in the air and my heart was pounding in my chest. Was this fear gripping my heart or lack of courage? I realized, in the mid-air of the Kakum Park walkway, that I preferred the feeling of safety to that of taking a risk.

I immediately turned around, determined to go back, but I had forgotten the instructions. Turning back was not allowed, as there were people behind us in a single line. Once the walkway had been started, you had to complete it. Even if you panicked halfway through, once the journey on the walkway had started, you just had to find the courage from within and press on to the end.

We all completed the journey in the end. I had no choice but to find the courage. There was the evidence of the people in front of us moving on. Our own children just ran across, enjoying the sway in the ropes. There were people coming behind us with confidence. So, I had to find a way to overcome this grip on my heart. Fear in the heart can be overcome by courage.

Courage is the quality that enables you to face your fears, disregard or overcome them, and tackle the goals in front of you. Courage helps you to be persistent in your forward movement. Courage prevents you from giving up in the face of your inner doubts. Courage will talk you out of going back on your dreams and vision. Courage keeps you fighting until the end-goal is in reach.

This quality is necessary when you begin the journey of fulfilling your destiny. There will be moments when you feel like it is safer to give up. There will be moments when the walkway appears to sway. There will be moments when you feel like there is not enough support around you – you feel vulnerable and exposed, like you are risking your life to complete the assignment. In these moments, find the courage from within. There are people who have gone ahead of you and completed their journey of destiny, with all the risks involved. There are others coming after you who will complete it too. There is enough evidence around you to persuade you not to cave in to fear. Every fear strewn along the path must be counteracted with courage.

Someone has defined fear with the acronym F.E.A.R. standing for False Evidence Appearing Real. When I was on the walkway, meters high in the air, the question that came into my mind was, *what will happen if the ropes snap?* The gentle sway appeared to me as evidence that the ropes were about to give way. False reasoning produced in me the fear which made me hesitate to go forward, until courage eventually took over.

When I had reached the end of the walkway, I found the whole experience a useful test of courage. When courage helps you to plunge into the challenges ahead of you and overcome them, you will find the experience exhilarating.

Courage flows from confidence

When we know God intimately, we are conscious that He is always with us, whether that is in the valleys of life or on the mountaintops. In the midst of our battles, He is with us and we know that we are not fighting alone. When we know that He is fighting with us, we are confident of victory and can therefore face any frightening enemy. David was able to tell Goliath that his impending fight with him was actually the Lord's battle (1 Samuel 17:47). In Isaiah 43:2 God promises us, "*When you pass through the waters, I will be with you; and through the rivers, they shall not overflow you. When you walk through the fire, you shall not be burned, nor shall the flame scorch you.*"

As we seek to fulfil our destiny, when resistance, storms and enemies threaten us along the way, we need to be certain of God's abiding presence with us. Knowing that He is with us makes us strong enough to battle. David faced bears, lions and Goliath (all terrifying prospects for any normal person) with courage and he defeated them, despite his youth. Like David, courage will make you rise to overcome your obstacles, storms and enemies. Courage is needed to fulfill God-given destiny.

The challenge of courage for Gideon

Gideon gave us a vivid example of a man with the type of courage needed to fulfill his God-given assignment. God asked him to lead an army of three hundred soldiers to face the Midianite army, who had thousands of soldiers. By doing this, Gideon showed that he had courage deeply embedded in his heart. Initially, he himself did not know that this courage was in him.

When the angel first appeared to Gideon he called him a "mighty man of valor". Gideon protested vehemently at the greeting and questioned the angel: where were the miracles of God he had heard about, if the Lord was with them? Wasn't it the Lord who brought them out of Egypt? The Bible says in Judges 6:14, "*Then the Lord turned to him and said 'Go in this might of yours, and you shall save Israel from the hand of the Midianites. Have I not sent you?'*"

The Lord saw something in the heart of Gideon, which is why He chose him to be the deliverer of Israel at that time. After many protestations, Gideon eventually agreed to do the job. He blew a trumpet and invited people to come and join him to go and fight the Midianites. Thirty-two thousand strong men volunteered and came to join him. What was the number of the Midianites that gathered to fight the Israelites? The Bible describes them in Judges 7:12: *"Now the Midianites and Amalekites, all the people of the East, were lying in the valley as numerous as locusts; and their camels were without number, as the sand by the seashore in multitude."* This was the size of the army that Gideon had to fight with his volunteer force.

But God began a pruning procedure with the thirty-two thousand volunteers. He told Gideon that his army was too big. When they had secured victory, they would begin thinking that they had done it all by themselves. So, first the Lord directed those who were afraid in their hearts to go back to their houses. Twenty-two thousand of them confessed immediately that they were afraid to go to fight the Midianites. I wonder why they came at all? Perhaps the sound of the trumpet or peer pressure from friends made them come forward to join Gideon's army. But in reality, their hearts were not in the right place for battle. They left Gideon at the first pruning process and ten thousand men remained.

The Lord was not finished yet, though. He took them to a brook and asked them to drink water. Those who lapped the water putting their hand to their mouth were only three hundred. Those were the people, God told Gideon, who were qualified to go to battle. Yet, the Midianites were as innumerable as locusts! Here comes the need for courage. For someone to lead just three hundred soldiers into battle to face an army of thousands is foolhardy to say the least. But that is the assignment to which God had called Gideon. His destiny in life was to be a judge of Israel and bring protection and prosperity to the nation. Fulfilling this destiny began with delivering Israel from the hands of the Midianites. For Gideon to follow God's instructions, he needed courage – supernatural courage. But God saw this courage in the heart of Gideon.

For some of us, starting a journey on the path of our destiny may be as daunting as Gideon facing the Midianites. When we look at the resources in our hands and compare it with what will come against us, we may not want to start the journey at all. However, it is the Lord who calls and points us to our destiny. With Him we should have the confidence to begin what He has laid upon our hearts to do.

Gideon had to have courage to go into battle. Likewise, we need courage in our hearts to begin to do what He has called us to do. We need courage for the journey of destiny. When we are pursuing our God-give destiny, even when the odds appear to be against us in the natural, we can muster courage and begin to do what He has called us to do.

1 John 4:13 says, *"Now this is the confidence that we have in Him ...."* Our confidence in Him releases courage in us. Courage is a byproduct of our confidence in Him. The more time we spend with Him the stronger our confidence becomes, and the more ready we are to tackle the burdens and calling He has given us.

How did the battle end for Gideon?

God arranged for Gideon to eavesdrop a conversation between two of the Midianite soldiers concerning their fear of Gideon. Judges 6:9-11 says,

"It happened on the same night that the Lord said to him, 'Arise, go down against the camp (of the Midianites), for I have delivered it into your hand. But if you are afraid to go down, go down to the camp with Purah your servant and you shall hear what they say; and afterward your hands shall be strengthened to go down against the camp.'"

When Gideon listened to the conversation, he discovered that one of them had had a dream in which God had delivered the Midianites, and their whole camp, into the hand of Gideon. This sparked up the light of courage in Gideon and he raised the war cry: *"Arise, for the Lord has delivered the camp of Midian into your hand."*

Using the noise of trumpets during the fight, the three hundred-strong army brought confusion to the camp of the Midianite army and put them to flight. Israel was delivered from the hands of the Midianites. Gideon began his reign as a judge of Israel.

Paul and courage

When Paul finally began to follow his God given destiny, he did not face a physical battle or an enemy like Goliath. Paul had to make an about-turn and declare that the Christians he had spent all his time persecuting were actually following the true God.

His conversion was so radical that within a couple of days he started preaching Christ in the synagogues. In Acts 9:21, we read, *"Then all who heard were amazed, and said, 'Is this not he who destroyed those who called on this name in Jerusalem, and has come here for that purpose, so that he might bring them bound to the chief priests?'"*

How could Paul face his former colleagues and tell them that Jesus was the Christ all along? This required courage. He needed courage to admit to those he had conspired with to attack the Christians, that they had been wrong to do so. That, from them on, he would no longer be with them, but would speak for the Lord Jesus and prove that He was, in fact, the Christ. He also needed to face the Christians and tell them that he was wrong for his past actions. He needed to join them and fellowship with them.

No wonder the Jews plotted to kill him. On the other hand, when he came to Jerusalem, the disciples shunned him when he tried to join them. But God had revealed Paul's calling and destiny to him. Now he just needed courage to begin his new journey, despite his past actions.

When our destiny becomes clear and undeniable to us, we require courage to overcome the initial doubts, skepticism, hatred, and the nay-sayers in our path. These could be many and powerful. In some cases, they may appear justified because of our past. But the discovery of destiny begins deep down in the heart. And, deep down in the heart we can still find the courage to begin the journey.

In Paul's case, he only realized much later that God had marked him out for his assignment from his mother's womb. Out of ignorance, blinded by the wrong training he had received in Judaism, he had fought against his own destiny. He tried to destroy that which he was called to live for. It took the direct intervention of the Lord Jesus Christ Himself on his way to Damascus to turn him around. With a powerful light blinding him and knocking him down, the Lord revealed Paul's calling and destiny. What he was destroying out of ignorance was the destiny he should fulfill.

Paul looked back and admitted that his destiny was marked for him from birth. If he had been raised in the right environment, or had the right teachers early on, he might have begun his true journey of teaching the truth of God earlier. He was not proud of his past. He told Timothy (1 Timothy 1:13) that because he did not pursue his true destiny from God in the beginning, he blasphemed and persecuted the way of the Gospel of Jesus Christ. He was violent and destroyed many believers and churches. But when the realization came to him, he was courageous enough to turn around and preach that Christ is the way of salvation. The right environment, the right association, and the right teachers can help you discover early on what the Lord has destined you for in life – but it is never too late.

Jonathan failed the test of courage

When David appeared on the scene as the conqueror of Goliath, he and Jonathan (son of Saul) had an immediate connection. 1 Samuel 18:1 reads, *"Now when he had finished speaking to Saul, the soul of Jonathan was knit to the soul of David, and Jonathan loved him as his own soul."* Maybe it was destiny that beckoned Jonathan to join David and help fulfill *his* God-given destiny? The irony was that the prophet Samuel had already declared that the Lord had chosen David to become king of Israel in place of Saul, Jonathan's father.

Samuel had anointed David as king. Nevertheless, Saul was not going to hand over the throne at the word of Samuel. Even though

Saul had no intention of handing over the throne to David, Jonathan loved the young and courageous man.

On several occasions king Saul tried to kill David to get rid of him, but Jonathan protected David from his father's assassination attempts and helped David to escape. One of the reasons why Saul wanted to kill David was so that his son Jonathan could succeed him. But it became clear to everyone that the hand of the Lord was on David for leadership and kingship.

When David was in exile, a fugitive from Saul, people began to flock to him. Those who believed there was a future for him as the next king of Israel joined him in exile. At one time he had an army of six hundred fighters around him in the wilderness. Even though Jonathan loved him and stood against his father for attempting to murder him, Jonathan could not leave the comforts of the palace to join David. He still stayed at his father's side.

While David was in hiding in the wilderness of Ziph, Jonathan visited him in the forest. This is what he told David in 1 Samuel 23:16-17: *"Then Jonathan, Saul's son, arose and went to David in the woods and strengthened his hand in God. And he said to him, 'Do not fear, for the hand of Saul my father shall not find you. You shall be king over Israel, and I shall be next to you. Even my father Saul knows that.'"*

Jonathan's statement to David was amazing! He told him that he would be king over Israel and that Jonathan would be beside him. Even his father knew of Jonathan's allegiance. If Jonathan was so sure that his covenant-friend would become king, then he could have joined him in the wilderness with the others. He even was more certain that he, Jonathan, would be sitting next to David when he became king. Destiny was beckoning Jonathan and he knew deep down in his heart that his place was next to David on the throne. However, it would take a significant level of courage to turn away from his father and follow what he knew was in his heart. Traditionally, as the first son of Saul, everyone expected him to be by the side of his father to help him maintain his throne.

So, Jonathan followed tradition and stayed to help his father, instead of following his destiny. He didn't have the courage to go against tradition and public expectation, even though he loved David so much. He wouldn't rebel against his upbringing, what he had been taught from childhood. The parental chord was too strong to cut loose. He still expected, however, that one day he would see the smooth transition of power from his father to David; that his friend would be invited to take the throne without Jonathan standing up for his destiny.

Unfortunately, the Philistines made war against Israel and the sons of Saul, including Jonathan, dutifully followed their father Saul into battle. The battle went against them and they were all killed on the same day. Jonathan died on Mount Gilboa. He was a man who knew in his heart that his place was to be by the side of his covenant-friend, David.

When destiny beckons you to step forward, you need to muster courage and follow what you know in your heart to be true. Sometimes your past life might haunt you, but with courage you can put it aside. Or, like Jonathan, you may need the force of courage to break with the traditions and expectations of men and do what you believe God is calling you to do.

Jonathan probably would have had a more exciting journey in life if he had followed the longing in his heart for David. David went on to become the greatest king ever known in Israel. If Jonathan had been by his side they could have achieved a lot together. Life would have been rewarding for Jonathan as well. He could have lived to impact his generation.

In the court of public opinion, a charge would have been laid on Jonathan that he had deserted his father and followed David. But Jonathan would have been fulfilling his destiny instead of dying on Mount Gilboa at the hands of the Philistines.

Be willing to go against public opinion when necessary. With courage you can break free from the prison of public opinion, if it stands in the way of you fulfilling God's destiny for your life.

Have courage

In Joshua 1:5-7, God commanded Joshua three times to be strong and courageous. "No man shall be able to stand before you all the days of your life. Just as was with Moses, so I will be with you. I will not leave you or forsake you. **Be strong and courageous**, for you shall cause this people to inherit the land that I swore to their fathers to give them. Only **be strong and very courageous**, being careful to do according to all the law that Moses my servant commanded you. Have I not commanded you? **Be strong and courageous**."

Saying it twice should have been enough, but God told Joshua three times to "be strong and courageous". Joshua had just been commissioned by God to fulfill the dream of all the Children of Israel, to take possession of the Promised Land. This was what Moses could not do, and Joshua was now discovering that it was his calling.

The book of Joshua opens with this statement: "Moses my servant is dead. Now therefore arise, go over this Jordan, you and this entire people ..." The Lord was calling Joshua to rise and take up the leadership position that Moses had left after his death. It was a tall order to fill Moses' shoes.

Moses had a rod of power in his hands. Through this rod, great miracles were wrought in Egypt. So much so that Moses was like a god in the eyes of Pharaoh. Exodus 7:1 says, "So the Lord said to Moses: 'See, I have made you as God to Pharaoh...'"

Look at some of the great things that God did through the hands of Moses. Moses stretched his hands and the Red Sea parted for the Children of Israel to pass through on dry ground. He stretched forth the rod again and the Red Sea came back together and swallowed up six hundred of Pharaoh's elite soldiers and their chariots. Under the leadership of Moses, the Children of Israel had manna falling from heaven every day, sufficient to feed all of them without any of them complaining that they had not had their fill. He brought water out of the rock for them to drink when they were thirsty. When his authority was challenged by Korah, Dathan, and Abiram, the earth opened up and swallowed this rebellious group and their families in a second. Their supporters, some two hundred and fifty men, were consumed by fire immediately. When his own brother Aaron and sister Miriam sought to correct him over marrying an Ethiopian woman, Miriam was immediately struck with leprosy and had to depend on Moses' intercession for her healing and restoration.

The Lord himself summed up the distinctness of Moses in these words in Numbers 12: 6:

"Hear now My words: If there is a prophet among you I the Lord, make Myself known to him in a vision; I speak to him in a dream; not so with My servant Moses; He is faithful in all My house. I speak with him face to face, even plainly, and not in dark sayings; and he sees the form of the Lord. Why then were you not afraid to speak against my servant Moses?"

The Lord said of Moses that he was faithful and that He spoke with him "face to face". Even his face shone when he prayed and fasted on the holy mountain for forty days and forty nights.

The invitation to Joshua

Now God was telling Joshua to fill those same shoes of leadership and do what Moses failed to do. Anyone who stopped to think about the enormity of such a task must naturally have doubted or been afraid. How could Joshua succeed where Moses had failed?

Most of us, when we weigh the enormity of what the Lord has for us to do, will need to meditate on God's message to Joshua about courage again and again.

If Joshua had cared to examine Moses' situation carefully, he would have realized that part of the reason Moses was unable to take the Children of Israel into the Promised Land was simply that they were stubborn. The Children of Israel regularly provoked God to anger with their ingratitude, disobedience and rebellion. Now, Joshua's assignment was to take the same Children of Israel into the Promised Land. The Lord told Joshua that the main qualities he needed to do this were strength and courage.

The Boldness Factor

We saw earlier how the prophet Samuel prepared Saul for the occasion of his introduction to Israel as their first king. They had detailed and fruitful discussions. Samuel called the nation together in Mizpah and prepared for lots to be cast, according to the usual procedure to discover the will of God. The lot fell on the tribe of Benjamin, signifying that the king would be divinely chosen from the tribe of Benjamin. After the tribe of Benjamin was chosen, Samuel began to cast lots family by family to see which family the lot would fall on, until eventually Saul was chosen.

Friend, the life lessons of many generations show that your destiny does not depend on how great your family background is. Your significance does not arise from the fact that you have a famous family, or one that no one has ever heard of. Trace the roots of many people who, in their lifetime, influenced society and affected nations and you will see that not many came from high-achieving families, or had a good start in life. Many came from the backside of the desert, or the poorest parts of our towns and villages. Nevertheless, once they stepped into their God-given destiny they began to excel.

Remember Saul's response to the prophet Samuel in 1 Samuel 9:21? *"Am I not a Benjamite, of the smallest of the tribes of Israel, and my family the least of all the families of the tribe of Benjamin?"*

The lot fell on the family of Matri, from which Saul came, to provide the king for Israel. It's interesting that this "least of all" family would have come to prominence above all the other families in Israel, because of Saul becoming king. You may come from a family that has lived in obscurity, but when you begin to fulfil your destiny, your family will rise with you.

We saw earlier that even though Samuel had adequately prepared Saul for his calling, he ran away into hiding. Fear gripped his heart and he could not bear the attention of the multitude. It is not enough to know what God's destiny is for your life – you must also have the force of *boldness* in your character to step forward and begin to fulfill it. Today, if you find yourself hiding, or refusing to step into public to do what you are called to do, may the Lord in His mercy and grace arrange circumstances to fish you out and pull you to where you really belong!

For you, reading this book, my prayer is that you will not just be taller than the people around you, but that you may have *boldness* in your heart to grasp your moments of destiny. David was a good example of someone with boldness in his inner man.

David's boldness

Sent as a messenger to take food to his elder brothers on the battlefield (1 Samuel 17:17), David encountered Goliath. He was taunting the Israeli army and hollering at their soldiers. "*Choose a man for you, and let him come down to me. If he is able to fight with me and kill me, then we will be your servants. But if I prevail against him and kill him, then you shall be our servants and serve us. I defy the armies of Israel this day; give me a man that we may fight together.*"

David heard these words and was stirred up with indignation. While the men of Israel fled in fear, the young David saw this as an opportunity to earn some reward. He asked the men of Israel, "*What shall be done for the man who kills this Philistine and takes away the reproach from Israel?*"

He wanted to know what the reward for would be the one who fought and killed Goliath. Upon being told that the king would give great riches, his daughter's hand in marriage, and exemption from all taxes in Israel, David boldly proclaimed that he was ready for the challenge! He would take Goliath on and earn the promised reward.

David was not invited to fight Goliath because he was young. He was not even part of Israel's fighting army. He was just on an errand when the opportunity to fight Goliath appeared. The opportunity to earn those rewards had been offered to all the fighting men of Israel but, whilst they cowered in fear and ran away from Goliath, David seized the moment and boldly announced his arrival on the stage of destiny. It took boldness in his heart, and a righteous indignation that an uncircumcised Philistine dared to defy the armies of Israel, for him to shout, "I am here!"

On the surface, it looked as though he was just interested in the rewards that the king offered. However, this single feat of facing and killing Goliath brought David into the limelight and set him on his journey of destiny as the next king of Israel. Before his family, and in his father's house, he was immediately anointed as king. No one apart from those present knew of this but, by coming out publicly and openly to defeat Goliath, soon the whole nation had heard of him. The stage was being set for his acceptance later as king. Boldness was the key for this young man.

In his moment of truth, Saul went into hiding among the travelling bags, but David exhibited the force of boldness and brought himself to the attention of a whole nation.

It is good to be bold in what you can do. Fear does not help anyone in this life.

Proverbs 28:1 says, *"The wicked flees when no one pursues, but the righteous are as bold as a lion."* May God give you the boldness of a lion as you seek to discover and step into a path leading you to fulfill your destiny!

10. Desire and Hunger

The Desire Factor

There are two men named Lazarus spoken of in the New Testament. The disciple John gave a vivid account of one in his Gospel. His life was full of meaningful relationship, drama, extraordinary miracles and relevance. When he got sick, the sisters sent a message to the Lord Jesus to come quickly and heal him. They simply said, *"Lord, behold, he whom You love is sick."* He had a good relationship with the Lord Jesus and though he died and was buried for four days, his friend Jesus raised him up from the dead. He certainly had a powerful testimony to tell all his life. His impact on his township and fellow Jews was so great that in John 12:9-10 the chief priests actually plotted to kill him. There was, however another Lazarus. A man who epitomizes a wasted life, not spent in the pursuit of God-given destiny. Luke wrote about him in Luke 16:19-31. He described him as a beggar who was full of sores, who lay at the gate of an unnamed rich man – someone who never cared about God, but lived a life of pleasure. This Lazarus could not take care of his physical body. Dogs licked his wounds and he was so weak he could not drive them away. He had no one to take care of him. He had not invested in relationships when he was well and younger. Furthermore, he was lying at the gate of a rich man waiting for leftover food. No wonder he was only surrounded by dogs. This is a picture of a wasted life: lying at somebody's gate waiting for leftovers. There was no direction to his life, no effort to live a better life, and no effort to make an impact on anyone at all.

Surprisingly, when he died, angels came to carry his spirit into Abraham's bosom. Angels were present at his death because he believed in God and had faith in Him. On the other hand, the rich man who was obviously a successful entrepreneur and enjoyed a life of pleasure in the flesh – partying, fashionable clothes, a large gated house – had no saving faith in God. Consequently, when he died, he went to hades, the place of suffering.

The irony in the lesson is this: how does a person who has a saving faith in God turn out to be a helpless beggar lying at the gate of someone who has no faith in God? How did it happen that a person with a saving faith had made no positive impact on his society? He had no fellowship or relationship with anyone else, yet the rich man, who did not care about God, always had guests in his house and was feasting sumptuously with others.

Lazarus the beggar appeared not to have lived a meaningful life prior to his introduction in Luke 16:19. He was a believer, but did not know what his destiny in life was. He had faith in the God of Abraham, but did not know what to do with his faith. He was alive, but did not know that he had to invest in relationship with others. He believed God for his salvation but did not know that there was a purpose and a God-given destiny for his life on earth.

The futility of his life is brought into sharp focus when we put the two Lazarus' side by side. They both had faith in God enough to be saved. But, the first Lazarus lived a life full of drama, miracles, relationship, and association with Jesus, making an impact on his generation. The second Lazarus had no desire for anything other than crumbs from the rich man's house. He just wanted each day's survival ration at the expense of someone else. There was no direction to his life and no desire for anything beyond getting through each day.

The psalmist cried out in Psalm 34:12, "*Who is the man who desires life, and loves many days, that he may see good?*" In this life, there must be a strong desire in you to live beyond just survival. To discover and fulfill your God-given destiny you must cultivate the desire for "life", and see good coming out of your existence on the earth. You must first believe that you are in the world to make a difference to your generation or the society in which you live. Desire life, find your destiny and fulfill it. Do not be like the second Lazarus, the beggar.

With saving faith in God and His Son Jesus Christ you will go to heaven when you die. Angels will be at your death bed to carry you away. But you would have wasted your life. Have a desire for real life!

Discipline is required

The psalmist provides the answer to his own question in Psalm 34:12, *"Who is the man who desires life?"* He points to discipline as the first requirement in such a person. He proclaims that such a person must, *"Keep your tongue from evil, and your lips from speaking deceit. Depart from evil and do good; seek peace and pursue it.*

The psalmist speaks about first exercising discipline over the tongue. Do not speak evil; do not run yourself down with negative comments. In Proverbs 18:20 the wise man said, *"A man's stomach shall be satisfied from the fruit of his mouth; from the produce of his lips he shall be filled. Death and life are in the power of the tongue, and those who love it will eat its fruit."*

On the path to discovering destiny, one needs to speak positively and in line with God's Word. Lazarus did not desire life beyond the crumbs from someone's table, probably because all he spoke about was his expectations of the crumbs for that day.

When the Lord Jesus met the lame man who had been lying at the pool of Bethesda for thirty-eight years (John 5), He asked him what it was that he really wanted. Did he *really* want to be made whole? The desire in your heart will influence the actions you take towards fulfilling your destiny. A lack of desire will immobilize you and keep you lying at someone else's gate looking for crumbs.

The Hunger Factor

In Genesis 25:29-32 we read that Esau was hungry for food but Jacob was hungry for spiritual blessing. Esau was the firstborn of the two brothers. According to the Jewish custom, he had to receive the firstborn blessing from his father. The firstborn's privileges also included a double portion of the inheritance of the father (Deuteronomy 21:17). We all experience moments when we suddenly become hungry and require food. Or perhaps we are occupied with an assignment and miss lunch or dinner. When we realize that mealtime has passed we get hunger pangs.

On that fateful day Esau, the elder son of Isaac, went to hunt in the forest. He was determined to make a good catch before returning home. Consequently, he came back home late in the day. Most probably he missed both breakfast and lunch. Late in the day, as he came home with hunger pangs, he approached his younger brother Jacob who had just prepared a bowl of lentil stew. The aroma of Jacob's food filled the air. Desperate to eat, he asked for a bowl of hot lentil stew to satisfy his hunger.

His brother, Jacob was like a predator, ready to pounce. At his brother's request for a bowl of lentil stew, Jacob demanded the price of Esau's firstborn blessing and rights. He demanded that Esau should forfeit his birthright, with all its privileges and rights, as well as the double share of his father's inheritance – all in exchange for a bowl of stew. What a lopsided deal! Isaac's properties would have included herds of cattle, farmlands, wells, dams, and servants!

Jacob comes across as a ruthless brother, but Esau was hungry and wanted to eat. In reality, two types of hunger are manifesting here. Jacob's proposal could not have been hatched on the spot. Jacob must already have been mulling over his lot in life. As the second born he was to inherit only one-third of his father's property and, as well as that, he was also missing out on the special blessing conferred on the first born. It was that blessing that Jacob was (rightly or wrongly) hungry for. He was hungry for his father's blessing, even though he was not entitled to it. On the other hand, Esau was simply hungry for food.

Jacob's proposition was not fair. Brothers ought to love each other, share everything freely and rejoice in each other's blessings. However, the unthinkable happened. Esau, with his agonizing hunger, thought,

"Look, I am about to die; so what is this birthright to me?" (Genesis 25:32)

"And Jacob gave Esau bread and stew of lentils; then he ate and drank, arose, and went his way. Thus Esau despised his birthright." (Genesis 25:34)

For a plate of lentil stew Esau sold his birthright blessings and inheritance to Jacob and satisfied his physical hunger. For a plate of lentil stew, Jacob bought the firstborn's blessing and inheritance and satisfied his hunger for more spiritual blessing. No wonder he got blessed again in place of Esau in Genesis 27. Both of them satisfied their hunger. One was for physical food and the other was for spiritual food. What are you hungry for in this life?

In discovering your God-given destiny, what you are hungry for matters. You will pay the price for what you are hungry for. If Esau had been hungry for spiritual blessing, then he would have tolerated his hunger pains and made his own food. Yet, he proved that his desires were selfish, worldly and just to satisfy his physical hunger.

It is necessary to identify what is really valuable to you in this life and be hungry for it. Without hunger for the valuable, specific blessings on your path of destiny, you will trade your destiny for some temporary satisfaction. When you are really hungry, you will pay the price required to get there.

What price is required from us today in our journey? Sacrifice, patience, humility and obedience to the Father.

Later in his life we see that Jacob, even though he was the younger of the two brothers, became the patriarch through whom the nation of Israel came into being. He was the father of the twelve tribes of Israel. This was because he was blessed by his father Isaac. He was blessed because he was so hungry for the blessing.

Jacob's hunger for spiritual blessing showed itself again when he met the angel of the Lord, with whom he wrestled in Genesis 32:24:

"Then Jacob was left alone; and a Man wrestled with him until the breaking of day. Now when he saw that he did not prevail against him,

he touched the socket of his hip; and the socket of Jacob's hip was out of joint as he wrestled with him. And he said, 'Let Me go for the day breaks.' But he said, 'I will not let You go unless You bless me!' … And He blessed him there."

Jacob's hunger for spiritual blessing was great. He made every effort to receive his father's blessing, and he refused to let this divine being go until he was blessed. The angel of the Lord could have knocked him out with his breath, but Jacob's determination was impressive.

Then, the angel of the Lord changed his name from Jacob to "Israel", which was in itself a blessing. *"And He said, 'Your name shall no longer be called Jacob, but Israel; for you have struggled with God and with men, and have prevailed.'"* Secondly, He pronounced a blessing on him. At the end of this encounter, Jacob's name had changed from Jacob (which means "deceiver") to Israel (which means "Prince with God").

In the New Testament, Esau was referred to as a profane person who despised his birthright. The difference between the impact that Esau and Jacob made on their generation, and the generations after them, can largely be attributed to what they were both hungry for in life. Your hunger determines the direction in which you will travel and the outcome of your life or the legacy you leave behind.

11. Diligence, Humility and Persistence

The Diligence Factor

Throughout the Scriptures, the Lord repeatedly told His people that they needed to be *diligent* in their worship. This means to be faithful, constant and wholly committed. He admonished them to not let go of what He had revealed to them about Himself. In Hebrews 11:6 we read, *"But without faith it is impossible to please Him, for he who comes to God must believe that He is, and that He is a rewarder of those who diligently seek Him."*

God wants us to seek Him *diligently*. He looks for diligence from us in whatever we are doing. He rewards us when we are diligent about Him. He is a rewarder. But He does not reward a sloppy half-hearted search for Him and His ways. When it comes to following our destiny, He does not require anything less from us. Destiny must be pursued diligently.

Some begin pursuing the path of their destiny with vim, vigor and zeal, but slowly let it fizzle out. They do not fuel and re-fuel their desire to do what they have been called to do. The desire to make a meaningful impact on your generation must be fueled as you go along this journey. The initial excitement to do what you are called to do in life can be great. However, the journey is never smooth. The initial excitement wears off easily and then we have to dig in, determining to stay on the path until we see results, fruit and harvest.

Samson started his journey in a controversial manner. He knew he was called to be a judge and a deliverer of Israel and he was given strict rules of engagement for his destiny. He must be a Nazirite and live a consecrated life. The strict rules given to his parents, which he had been trained in from his childhood, included no alcohol or similar drink, no shaving of the hair, and that he should not eat anything unclean. Although diligent in living a consecrated life, Samson's one flaw was women. It should have gone without saying that a Nazirite could not live an immoral life, yet Samson fell in love with Delilah and that was his downfall. Delilah succeeded in shaving his hair and thereby robbed him of his strength from the Lord. He was overcome by the Philistines and locked up in prison.

To succeed in fulfilling our destiny, we must know exactly what the Lord has asked us to do. This requires diligent lifetime study. Leaving it to the assumption that once we know what the Lord has destined for us, we will automatically fulfill it, will not do. When he was locked up in prison, Samson found out too late. He did not know the full scope of what he had been called to, as judge and deliverer of Israel.

When David was anointed by the prophet Samuel to be king, the Lord orchestrated for him to spend some time in the court of king Saul. Before Saul eventually died and left the throne vacant, he sent for young David to serve in his palace. David was taken to Saul's palace first because of his musical skills and his ability to create an atmosphere in which evil spirits could not survive. He was invited there to minister deliverance to the king through his music and worship. However, this gave David the opportunity to observe and learn first-hand about the customs and protocols of the king's court. Sure enough, because he knew he had been anointed to be king one day, he did not only minister deliverance but also observed how the role of king worked.

Before that, most of David's time would have been spent caring for his family's flock of sheep. He was a shepherd boy and did not have a royal upbringing. He was ruddy and vibrant. He acted spontaneously and probably had little knowledge of the royal court. Yet, God called him to be king through His prophet Samuel. That was what God had destined for David. It is noteworthy to see that before he was enthroned, the Lord had set him up to serve in the king's court for a while. It was a time of learning for him.

Even when Saul was anointed as king, the prophet Samuel had to teach him and the people of Israel, "the behavior of royalty". 1 Samuel

10:25 says, *"Then Samuel explained to the people the behavior of royalty, and wrote it in a book and laid it up before the Lord."* There is always a learning process in whatever the Lord has called you to do. Diligence is required to learn all about the particular assignment He has for you. When you observe and learn, you will be in a good position to move forward.

Diligence is required for the long haul!

Anna the prophetess

There are two vivid examples of diligence, commitment and persistence in the New Testament. The period between Malachi and the New Testament was about 400 years. During this period there was no prophetic voice in Israel. The "fullness of time" for the Savior to be born was approaching. In His divine order, the Lord called some people to an intercessory life – to pray for the coming of the promised Messiah into the world. Before the Lord Jesus was born, God positioned two special intercessors in Israel – Simeon and Anna the prophetess – to intercede for His coming into the world. This was their assignment; the destiny that the Lord had prepared and called them into. Let us consider the diligence they exhibited as they approached their God-given destinies.

Luke 2:36-37 says, *"Now there was one, Anna, a prophetess, the daughter of Phanuel, of the tribe of Asher. She was of a great age, and had lived with a husband seven years from her virginity; and this woman was a widow of about eighty-four years, who did not depart from the temple, but served God with fasting and prayers night and day. And coming in that instant she gave thanks to the Lord, and spoke of Him to all those who looked for redemption in Jerusalem."*

Her destiny was to be an intercessor who would usher in the arrival of the incarnate son of God on the world stage. How did she approach this calling? She served God with fasting and prayer night and day for about sixty years.

She had lost her husband after seven years of marriage, whom she had lived with from her virginity. Assuming she married around the age of twenty-one, she became a widow at the age of twenty-eight. She did not marry again but gave herself to fulfilling her God-given destiny – an intercessor who would herald the birth of the Lord Jesus into the world! She did this until she was eighty-four years old!

When Joseph and Mary came into the temple to dedicate their baby son, Jesus, forty days after His birth, according to Mosaic Law (Leviticus 12:2-8), Anna came into the temple as she had faithfully done every day. Led by the Spirit, she began to talk about the baby Jesus as the One they were waiting for; as the Messiah. She faithfully interceded with fasting and prayer until her eyes beheld the Savior in person. What diligence she showed in fasting and praying night and day, coming to the temple to behold the baby after over fifty years of intercession. She was diligent in fulfilling what she knew was her destiny. Diligence means you will not give up halfway. Diligence will keep you going to the end.

Simeon

Luke 2:25-26 says, "And behold, there was a man devout in Jerusalem whose name was Simeon, and this man was just and devout, waiting for the consolation of Israel, and the Holy Spirit was upon him. And it had been revealed to him by the Holy Spirit that he would not see death before he had seen the Lord's Christ."

Simeon was waiting for the Messiah of Israel and the world to be born, spending his days in prayer and intercession, watching for the signs of His arrival. However hopeless the spiritual climate around us appears to be, intercessors doing their work with all diligence can provoke a breakthrough of light around us. This is what Simeon did so diligently. In the process of such diligent pursuit, the Lord revealed to him by the Spirit that he would not see death until he had seen the Lord Jesus in person.

The day he came into the temple and saw the baby in the arms of Mary was the day he knew he had fulfilled his destiny. He was quietly but diligently praying. Like Anna the prophetess, he was not discouraged by the confused teachings of the Pharisees and Sadducees of the day. He did not despair over how long it took for the Savior to be born, nor how heaven was silent during this period. He fulfilled his destiny and his eyes actually saw the Messiah. On the day that Joseph and Mary came to dedicate the baby Jesus, the Spirit of God led him to go to the temple. His heart was probably throbbing as the Lord revealed to him, opening his eyes to see, that the baby in the arms of Mary was the consolation of Israel.

Just as Anna the prophetess and Simeon were diligent in fulfilling their destinies, you and I are called to pursue our God-given destiny with diligence.

Knowing, or having a sense of the direction in which the Lord wants you to travel, is not enough. Fulfilling your destiny is what counts, and you need diligence, courage, and commitment to see it through.

Receiving help to fulfill destiny

A true God–given destiny, when it is fully revealed, is always overwhelming. It always seems impossible with the resources and energy that we have. Yet, when God gives a destiny, He provides all we need to fulfill it, and that often means receiving the help of others.

Nehemiah received help

Nehemiah was aware of the heavy burden on his heart to see the restoration of Jerusalem and the walls of the city rebuilt, but where were the resources going to come from? Even before he started, he needed permission to leave the palace of King Artaxerxes. As a captive in exile, how could he get the king to release him? It seemed impossible. Yet, without doing a thing, the pagan king noticed the burden on his heart and asked him what was wrong. When he told the king about his burden, the king simply asked him, "What do you request?"

Nehemiah shows us how we need to depend on the Lord every step of the way. Today, we would have been quick to catalogue everything we needed to do the task. But this is what Nehemiah recorded of himself in response to the king's question: *"So I prayed to the God of heaven"* (Nehemiah 2:4).

Before he did a thing, he prayed to God to guide him on what to say. He was standing before the king and conversing with him, but in the twinkling of an eye, he prayed and listened to God. Out of the Spirit's connection in that moment he was able to answer, and specifically asked the king to send him to Judah for the re-building process. He then went on and asked for exactly what he needed – timber etc. The release of everything Nehemiah needed began. His prayer gave him favor before the king. He had so much favor that the king provided him with captains of the army and horsemen to protect him.

When we pray to God in total dependence on His guidance and help, the Lord provides us with people who can help. These could be people in positions of authority or just ordinary people who come along. Help can come from unlikely sources. You would imagine King Artaxerxes would be the last person to be concerned about rebuilding the walls of Jerusalem, let alone the restoration of the glory and dignity of the people of Judah. He was the king of Babylon, whose predecessor had taken the Jews into captivity! But when it is God who has fashioned such a destiny, He brings the most unlikely people around us to help.

Expect helpers! They will be positioned on your way to help you as you pray and look to God to do the impossible. Some helpers will come with the resources you need to accomplish what He has laid on your heart.

Barnabas helped Paul

Paul was an example of someone who got to know his God-given destiny clearly, but needed the help of others to fulfill it. Paul's conversion on the road to Damascus was so radical that he immediately began to preach that the Lord Jesus was the Christ, the Son of God. This generated tension in two opposite camps. His fellow Jewish zealots suddenly wanted to kill him for undermining their mission, and the disciples of the Lord Jesus Christ would not allow him to join them because they didn't trust him and were afraid of him. Acts 9:26 reports that, *"And when Saul had come to Jerusalem, he tried to join the disciples; but they were all afraid of him, and did not believe that he was a disciple."*

Paul needed help.

Sure enough a helper showed up. Acts 9:27 states that, *"Barnabas took him and brought him to the apostles. And he declared to them how he had seen the Lord on the road, and that He had spoken to him, and how he had preached boldly at Damascus in the name of Jesus. So he was with them at Jerusalem, coming in and going out."*

Barnabas came to the rescue of Paul. He paved the way for the apostles to accept him as a genuine convert and, instead of being rejected, he was now accepted by the brethren.

God has helpers on the way for you in your efforts to pursue the path He has fashioned for you. Barnabas was described as a "son of encouragement". He was an encourager. At this time Paul desperately needed encouragement to weather the storms of the backlash from the zealot group.

For those of us who make a radical about-turn to follow our God-given destiny, God is faithful to send us helpers. He lines up our path with various types of helpers. Our responsibility is simply to recognize them and receive them as God-sent.

While Nehemiah received help from a powerful king, Barnabas was simply there to open the door for Paul to be accepted and endorsed by the Christian community. That was the help he needed. God may position people on your path who will bring you what you need at exactly the right time. This simple, perfectly timed help could be worth a lifetime of labor.

When Apollos wanted to go to Achaia to minister, it was Aquila and Priscilla who wrote letters of introduction for him, opening the door to the Christian community there for him.

The Lord will send you help

The psalmist said in Psalm 20:1-2, "May the Lord answer you in the day of trouble; may the name of the God of Jacob defend you; may He send you help from the sanctuary, and strengthen you out of Zion."

And Psalm 121:1 says, "I will lift up my eyes to the hills – from whence comes my help? My help comes from the Lord, who made heaven and earth."

When you decide to follow the path that God has put before you, the Lord will send you help. Often that help will come from the most unlikely source.

Joash helped save Gideon

When an angel of the Lord appeared to Gideon to reveal to him that he was going to deliver Israel from the hands of the Midianites, Gideon was terrified. The Lord had to reassure him: "Peace be with you; do not fear, you shall not die." With this assurance, and many others, Gideon began to carry out the instructions that the angel of the Lord gave him. The first instruction was that he should tear down the altar of Baal that belonged to his father and cut down the wooden image that was beside it. When he carried out this instruction, the following day the men of the city rose up early in the morning and enquired who had torn down the altar of Baal and the wooden image. On learning that it was Gideon, they decided that he should die immediately. Judges 6:30 says, "Then the men of the city said to Joash, 'Bring out your son, that he may die, because he has torn down the altar of Baal, and because he has cut down the wooden image that that was beside it.'"

For carrying out the instructions of the angel, the men of the city sentenced Gideon to death. The irony of the whole situation was that the evil altar of Baal belonged to Gideon's father. His father had to enforce the rules and Gideon knew the implications of tearing it down, so for that reason, he did it in the middle of the night when no one was watching. Judges 6:27 states that "…But because he feared his father's household and the men of the city too much to do it by day, he did it by night."

He took ten men from among his servants to help him cut down the structures. It must have been some elaborate structure containing the altar and the wooden image to require ten men to assist Gideon. With ten men involved it would be difficult to keep it secret. It was easy for the men of the city to investigate who was behind this. Now Gideon was facing death.

Where was the angel of the Lord who gave him the instruction? The angel had gone back to heaven and here was Gideon facing the wrath of the men of the city. Perhaps the angel would show up and release fire to save Gideon? No, for God's ways are not our ways. Isaiah 55:8 says, *"For My thoughts are not your thoughts nor are your ways my ways, says the Lord."*

The angel did not return to save Gideon from being lynched by the men of the city. However, Gideon did receive help. Gideon's own father, the owner of the altar of Baal, decided to save his son. He changed the rules immediately. He said that Baal should plead his own case. *"If he is a god, let him plead for himself, because his altar has been torn down"* (Judges 6:31). In other words, he ruled that no one should touch Gideon, but let Baal punish him if he is a god.

This is help from the most unlikely source. Joash was the owner of this altar. It was Joash who should have been seeking revenge. Gideon was already afraid that his father's household would rise against him if he touched the altar. But look at how help came through the very man whose altar was destroyed.

God can send us help through men. If Gideon had run to the field looking for an angel to miraculously save him from his predicament, he would have been disappointed. Help had already been provided by God in the very house in which he was residing. In fulfilling our God-given destiny, we need to be open, receptive and recognize the helpers that the Lord sends our way. God can send help to you from the most unlikely and unexpected sources. He can even use your enemies to help you fulfill your destiny.

Some have unknowingly despised those whom the Lord has sent to them. Some have turned them away. *"Go away we do not need you!"*

Isaac could have helped Abimelech, king of Gerar. Instead when they saw Isaac's prosperity, they chose to ask him to go away from them.

Some have turned away their God-sent helpers out of pride. "If God wants to help me, He will do it by a miracle," they say to themselves. But God sends help to us in His own way and sometimes that is through men and women we would least expect to support our cause. Recognize and receive them; and God's help through them will move you on to fulfill your destiny.

The young helpers and assistants

God also sends younger assistants to us as helpers to accomplish our God-given journey. Some come to us to learn; others to come to serve and assist us. They do not necessarily come with material assistance or to offer encouragement, or from a powerful position. They are just happy to be around us and, in the process of helping, they are mentored. Someone who was happy to be around a man of destiny was Elisha. There was no way Elijah could convince him to turn back and leave him alone.

On the other hand, at Pamphylia, the young John Mark decided to return to Jerusalem when he was accompanying Paul and Barnabas on their second missionary journey (Acts 13:13). Obviously, Paul was highly displeased with him and refused to take him back when he returned (Acts 15:36-39). Paul was adamant that anyone who proved unable to do a difficult journey should not be given a second chance. However, in his later years, Paul admitted that the young assistants were helpful to his mission after all. He sent for John Mark on the basis of his usefulness to him. "Get Mark and bring him with you, for he is useful to me for ministry" (2 Timothy 4:11).

Don't despise young helpers and assistants. They may be God-sent to help you fulfill your destiny.

The Holy Spirit, our ultimate Helper

The Lord Jesus said in John 14:25, "These things I have spoken to you while being present with you. But the Helper, the Holy Spirit, whom the Father will send in My name, He will teach you all things, and bring to your remembrance all things that I said to you."

Our ultimate Helper is the Holy Spirit. He is the One who is able to reveal to us what the Father has called us to. He is the One who can guide us on the journey: where to pass, where to turn, where to stop and where not to go. He warned Paul not to preach in Asia (Acts 16:6). He stopped Paul from going into Bithynia. He led them to go into Macedonia where they were beaten up and thrown into jail.

But the Holy Spirit is our ultimate guide in life. He is the revealer of the mind of God to us. As the third person in the Godhead, He knows the beginning from the end. He knew how the journey of Paul and Silas would turn out. Naturally speaking, I would have said that Paul and Silas should preach everywhere a door was opened to them. The door was open to them in Asia, but the Holy Spirit forbade them to go there because He wanted them in Macedonia, specifically in Philippi. He knew they would be thrown into jail, but He wanted a revival in the jail – for the prisoners to experience freedom and deliverance from sin. In addition, He wanted the jailer himself and his whole household to be saved. So, He led them through inner promptings, visions and dreams and brought them to Philippi. This is exciting isn't it? When we also learn how to recognize the leading of the Holy Spirit, our journey will become exciting and fulfilling. But we need to lean on the Holy Spirit and be led by Him. We need to trust Him even when the path looks bleak. He is here to help, He knows the way, He will show us how to overcome.

A lifelong commitment to destiny

Fulfilling one's destiny on earth is a lifelong journey. It was Paul who, in his final days, could say confidently that, "I have finished the race, I have kept the faith. Finally, there is laid up for me the crown of righteousness, which the Lord, the righteous Judge will give me on that Day, and not to me only but also to all who loved His appearing."

This journey unfolds progressively. The experiences of Paul attest to this. This is what the Lord told him on the way to Damascus (probably during his three days of prayer and fasting):

"But rise and stand on your feet; for I have appeared to you for this purpose, to make you a minister and a witness both of the things which you have seen and of the things **which I will yet reveal to you**. I will deliver you from the Jewish people, as well as from the Gentiles, to whom I now send you, to open their eyes, in order to turn them from darkness to light, and from the power of Satan to God, that they may receive forgiveness of sins and an inheritance among those who are sanctified by faith in Me."

There will be more assignments that the Lord will reveal to us, more challenges, more hindrances and more unforeseen battles on the journey. Nehemiah started with a burden to rebuild the walls of Jerusalem and restore its glory. Once he had completed the walls, he was faced with the problem of social injustice as the nobles and rulers among them enslaved the poor and took over their lands. He resolved this issue, then he was faced with the problem of reintroducing the reading of the Law. Then he had to encourage a spiritual revival… More and more challenges confronted him along the way. He successfully rose to the task on each occasion. This was because he had a lifelong commitment to his destiny, and his part in seeing the restoration of Jerusalem and Judah. He was simply a cup-bearer with a burden from the Lord to see the walls of Jerusalem and the dignity of his people restored, but his commitment to this goal was lifelong.

Paul spoke of some of his challenging life experiences in 2 Corinthians 11:24:

"From the Jews five times I received forty stripes minus one. Three times I was beaten with rods; once I was stoned; three times I was shipwrecked; a night and a day I have been in the deep; in journeys often, in perils of waters, in perils of robbers, in perils of the Gentiles, in perils in the city, in perils in the wilderness, in perils in the sea, in perils among false brethren; in weariness and toil, in sleeplessness often, in hunger and thirst, in fastings often, in cold and nakedness – besides the other things, what comes upon me daily; my deep concern for all the churches."

When the Lord revealed to him what he had called Paul to, He didn't tell him about receiving thirty-nine lashes, being beaten, stoned or shipwrecked. How would Paul have felt if he'd known from the beginning all that would befall him in fulfilling his destiny?

How would we feel if we knew all we'd have to go through in order to see our destiny fulfilled? Perhaps some would consider the price too high. What kept Paul going through all his harrowing difficulties? What will keep us going today? A lifelong commitment is required. Once we are confident that this is what the Lord requires of us, we have to live for that cause till our last breath on planet earth.

God does not desire us to partially complete our mission – He wants us to make it all the way to the end. The Lord Jesus puts it this way in Mark 8:34:

"When He had called the people to Himself, with His disciples also, He said to them, 'Whoever desires to come after Me, let him deny himself, and take up his cross and follow Me.'"

Fulfilling your God-given destiny will mean giving everything up to the Lord. This isn't a hobby or a fun pastime. God is asking you to take up your cross and follow Him. But have no fear, He will be with you along the way and will never leave you.

"Looking unto Jesus, the author and finisher of our faith…" (Hebrews 12:2)

12. Overcoming the Destiny Stoppers

It should be thrilling to finally know the destiny God has fashioned for you in this life. People who know they are on the path to their destiny give their all to it. It becomes their heartbeat. They have a passion for what they are doing, knowing that this is what God has called them to. They enjoy what they do knowing that their reward is in the fulfillment of their destiny.

However, we have all seen people who knew their destiny, started on the path, then got lost or distracted. They seemed to get in a fog and eventually lost their way, settling for something less. So, we cannot talk about discovering and fulfilling our destiny without talking about the *destiny stoppers*. These are powerful forces that fight us when we seek to fulfill our God-given destiny. After the initial thrill of knowing what God wants us to do, they swoop in and employ all kinds of means to weaken and discourage us.

On our journey we may meet any of the following four groups of destiny stoppers:

a) Resistance, Hurdles and Obstacles

b) Distractions, Discouragement and Disobedience

c) Sin and Deception

d) Demonic Stoppers and Forces of Darkness

While God sends us help to enable us to accomplish what He has called us to, we also have an enemy who is set against us. The devil wants us to be frustrated and discontented. Once we begin our God-appointed journey, we are a threat to his kingdom, and he will raise up all kinds of storm and resistance against us.

When the Lord Jesus invited His disciples to get into the boat and go to the other side of the Sea of Galilee on a mission, a great storm arose while they were on the way (Mark 4:35-40). Although the Sea of Galilee was only eight miles wide and crossing it should not have been difficult for professional fishermen like Peter, James, Andrew and others, the storm was so severe that the disciples had to wake Jesus up and cry to Him that they were perishing. The Lord Jesus had to rise and rebuke the storm. By using His authority in such a way, it was clear that the origin of the storm was the devil. He was attempting to stop the Lord and the disciples from going to the Gadarenes region where He would deliver a demon-possessed man. They were on a mission that would eventually impact the whole Decapolis region.

The demoniac who was delivered on that mission later prepared the way for the Lord Jesus coming to the region. By the time the Lord Jesus came again to the Decapolis (Mark 7:31), the whole region was ready to receive Him and there were great miracles of healing and revival. That mission was so crucial and strategic to the kingdom of God that the devil was stirred to attack.

When *you* have a destiny that is going to impact the world positively, do not be surprised when the devil comes against you with all kinds of storms, resistance, hurdles and obstacles. He wants to stop you from achieving your dreams; he doesn't sit back and look on as you go out to impact society in the name of Jesus Christ.

Look at Paul's life and the resistance he came up against as he went out preaching the Gospel. In 2 Corinthians 11:23-27 we read,

"I am more in labors more abundant, in stripes above measure, in prisons more frequently, in deaths often. From the Jews five times I received forty stripes minus one. Three times I was beaten with rods, once I was stoned; three times I was shipwrecked; a night and a day I have been in the deep; in journeys often, in perils of my own countrymen, in perils of the Gentiles, in perils in the city, in perils in the wilderness, in perils in the sea, in perils among false brethren; in weariness and toil, in sleeplessness often, in hunger and thirst, in fastings often, in cold and nakedness…"

Obviously, the majority of these obstacles and persecutions were inspired by the devil to stop Paul from doing what God had called him to do. But Paul's focus was the end-goal. He was determined to fulfill the destiny God had called him to, so he did not allow anything to deter him. He wasn't discouraged and didn't fall into despair. This should be our attitude today if we want to fulfill God's destiny for our lives.

When we read the accounts of Paul's persecutions, it becomes clear that we will need God's supernatural grace to persevere to the end.

In Lystra, Paul was stoned and left for dead! This was after he had preached and healed a lame man. The Jews from Antioch and Iconium came to Lystra and stirred up the crowd against Paul and Barnabas (Acts 14:19). Instead of rejoicing that a man, lame from his mother's womb, was healed, they stoned Paul until they believed he was dead and left him on the ground. The Christians in Lystra came and encircled him (presumably to pray) and Paul rose up. The next day he went to the next city, Derbe, and continued preaching.

We may well have despaired of such a mission. Shouldn't Paul have allowed himself a day or two's break, to recover? No, he pressed ahead. Such persecutions and attacks were designed to wear him out and lead him to give up, but Paul persisted and persevered.

Persistence and faithfulness are the qualities that kept him going. The same attitude will keep you going when you come against satanic attacks. Paul's eyes were fixed on the end result and not on the resistance or obstacles. He saw them as light afflictions that could be overcome. He saw them in the same way as David. In 2 Samuel 22:29-30 David penned this prophetic song: *"For You are my lamp, O Lord; The Lord shall enlighten my darkness. For by You I can run against a troop; by my God I can leap over a wall."* And in verse 35 he said, *"He makes my feet like the feet of a deer, and sets me on my high places. He teaches my hands to make war, so that my arms can bend a bow of bronze."*

Just as David saw himself leaping over the obstacles and hindrances on his path, we should see ourselves leaping over whatever the devil sets against us today. Do not stop or go back simply because you have come across a tall wall blocking your path. You can leap over it!

A divine strategy is available

After Israel had crossed the River Jordan in Gilgal, Joshua went to observe the tall walls of Jericho. He wondered how they could climb these walls, or get through them to attack the city within. As he stood, gazing at the walls, he beheld a Man standing opposite him with His sword drawn in His hands. Joshua 4: 13-15 says, *"And Joshua fell on his face to the earth and worshipped, and said to Him, 'What does my Lord say to His servant?'"* After this encounter with the Lord, God gave Joshua the strategy to bring the walls down and take over the city of Jericho.

"See! I have given Jericho into your hand, its king, and the mighty men of valor. You shall march around the city, all you men of war; you shall go all around the city once. This you shall do six days. And seven priests shall bear seven trumpets of rams' horns before the ark. But the seventh day you shall march around the city seven times and the priests shall blow the trumpets. It shall come to pass, when they make a long blast with the ram's horn, and when you hear the sound of the trumpet that all the people shall shout with a great shout; then the wall of the city will fall down flat. And the people shall go up every man straight before him." (Joshua 6:2-5)

The Lord has the perfect strategy for you, too, when you come upon hindrances, hurdles and obstacles. Here, Joshua was met by the Lord Himself, already in battle mode. He introduced Himself as the Commander of the army of the Lord and, just like Joshua, as you worship God, the Commander of your destiny, He will come and reveal to you the strategy to overcome any obstacles in your destiny-path.

Learn to honor and worship Him in moments of perplexity and confusion. When you are overwhelmed seek His face. Just wait on the Lord with confident expectation. He told Joshua *"Take your sandal off your foot, for the place where you stand is holy"* (Joshua 5:15). As you worship Him, you will hear His voice. Let Him be in command of your destiny.

We thank God that He gives us the strength and strategies to overcome the devil. However, the devil is not the only source of opposition to us fulfilling our destiny. We can become our own worst enemy when we allow ourselves to be distracted from the journey, or become discouraged by the nature of the assignment the Lord has given us. Also, when we choose to disobey the voice of the Lord we may find ourselves wandering in the wilderness and frustrating our own progress. This, of course, will greatly affect the impact we could have in the area the Lord has called us to minister.

Distraction from the enemy in our camp!

Samson had let his guard down. He was lying on Delilah's lap, sound asleep. Judges 16:19-21 reads,

"Then she lulled him to sleep on her knees, and called for a man and had him shave off the seven locks of his heard. Then she began to torment him, and his strength left him. And she said 'The Philistines are upon you, Samson!' So he awoke from his sleep and said 'I will go out as before, at other times, and shake myself free!' But he did not know that the Lord had departed from him. Then the Philistines took him and put out his eyes, and brought him down to Gaza. They bound him with bronze fetters, and he became a grinder in the prison."

Because Samson could not discipline himself in his sexual conduct, he let the enemy in. God had called him to be a judge a deliverer of Israel, a Nazirite, consecrated to the Lord, and this one area in his life was his downfall.

His first desire for a Philistine woman was intriguing. He demanded that his parents get him a Philistine woman in Timnah to marry. His parents were against it and dissuaded him from marrying a lady from the enemy's camp. His second entanglement was with a harlot, a prostitute. His third entanglement was with the Philistine woman Delilah. This was no marriage, but a long affair. For a man whose glorious destiny was revealed by an angel, Samson seemed to take his calling for granted.

Throughout the period of the affair, Delilah sought to discover the source of strength in order to betray him to the Philistines. Delilah did not love him, she was in it for the money. By losing his supernatural strength, Samson's destiny would be aborted. Yet Samson kept on the affair with Delilah, even though he knew that Delilah was setting a trap for him.

At first glance, it appears that Delilah was the enemy. Yet the more dangerous enemy was the one within Samson himself. He needed to discipline himself and realize the enormity of what God had given him. He needed to honor God and revere the calling and destiny of his life. No one could impose this discipline on Samson but himself.

Likewise, no one can impose on another the discipline required to fulfill a God-given destiny. Self-discipline comes from within. After understanding our destiny, we need to be wholly separated to the Lord and His will. We need to live for that cause. In John 18:37 Jesus said to Pontius Pilate, "*For this cause I was born, and for this cause I have come into the world, that I should bear witness to the truth.*"

We must know the cause for which we were born and we must live for that cause. Samson knew the cause for which he was born but did not understand that it was not only obeying the three rules of the Nazirite vow. Rather, it meant living totally separated to the Lord.

We need to be separated to the Lord. What does this mean? To be *in* the world but not *of* the world. By living this way, our lives will have an impact and be a blessing to those whom the Lord has placed within our sphere. But this will mean conquering the enemy within us, through discipline. Wrongful desires, or desires that lead us away from God, should be crucified on the altar of consecration.

From a deliverer to a grinder

Samson lost his supernatural strength – the tool of deliverance and his destiny – on the lap of Delilah. The Philistines took out his eyes, bound him with bronze fetters and imprisoned him. In prison he became a grinder – perhaps grinding corn or cereals for food for the other prisoners. Here is a man with a glorious destiny, shackled by chains and working as a slave.

The distraction of sexual immorality has changed the course of many people's lives. It is a low blow the devil gives, but the real enemy is within us. With discipline, separation unto the Lord, and a consecrated life, we will not be distracted and stumble from our true course.

Gehazi's lust for material things

Gehazi, a servant of Elisha, had a great opportunity in life. That opportunity was great because of who Elisha was, and how Elisha became a prophet.

After watching his master for some time, Elisha had greatly desired that one day he should receive an impartation from Elijah to carry on his work, with signs and wonders. Before his departure into heaven, Elijah asked him what he wanted, and Elisha boldly asked for an impartation of double the anointing that was on Elijah. Elijah told him that this was a hard thing he was asking. Nevertheless he gave him a double impartation.

Eventually, Elisha picked up the mantle of Elijah and the miracles recorded in his ministry were indeed twice those of Elijah's. Elisha knew the values of impartation, about how a servant could receive double what their masters carried. Therefore, it was a great privilege for Gehazi to be a servant of Elisha. Gehazi was in pole position to receive a mighty impartation from Elisha and carry on a great prophetic ministry, potentially double what Elisha had carried!

However, as we will see, greed was the enemy within Gehazi.

After Elisha had healed Naaman, the Syrian army commander, from leprosy, Naaman attempted to repay him with a gift. He begged Elisha to receive an offering from him. Gehazi was standing by and, to his shock and horror, his master turned down the gift and told him in effect, "Go in peace, healed for free, at no cost." (Compare that with some in the prophetic field today who charge consultation fees for a prayer time!) We must bow our heads in humility at the example of Elisha, ministering freely to Naaman and refusing to receive a gift.

Like those commercial prophets today, Gehazi was horrified at the lost opportunity of receiving a gift. He ran after Naaman and told him a lie. He said he had been sent by Elisha, who had changed his mind and now wanted a talent of silver and two changes of garments from him. Naaman had already begged to give an offering, so he was delighted to do it and happily gave Gehazi two talents of silver in two bags and two changes of garments.

Gehazi witnessed miracles. He was ministering in a supernatural atmosphere and being prepared to receive a great impartation. But greed was within him. Greed for money, clothing and other material things. The greed was so overpowering that he was prepared to tell a blatant lie concerning his master. It was foolhardy for anyone walking with a prophet like Elisha to attempt to tell a lie, but the greed in Gehazi was so great that he was no longer afraid of being discovered.

By the time he had hidden all the things in his house, Elisha called him and asked a simple question: "Where did you go, Gehazi?" He could either confess or tell another lie. He chose to lie again.

The opportunity for Gehazi to be faithful and receive a powerful impartation from his master was wasted because of greed and deceit. The end result was the judgment that Elisha pronounced on him. In 2 Kings 5:26-27 Elisha tells him, *"Did not my heart go with you when the man turned back from his chariot to meet you? Is it time to receive money and to receive clothing, olive groves, vineyards, sheep and oxen, male and female servants? Therefore the leprosy of Naaman shall cling to you and your descendants forever."* And he went out from his presence leprous, as white as snow.

Following your God-given destiny is much more important than any material possession or temporary gratification. Do not be distracted by these things. Whatever you sacrifice now will eventually be compensation for as you remain faithful. Remember, there is time for everything. Elisha's point to Gehazi was not that receiving gifts was wrong, but that it was *not the time* to receive gifts from this particular Gentile. Let him go home free, healed of leprosy, knowing that God is good!

Paul, in his epistle to the Philippians, lamented of Christians who, at one time, were in his ministry team but had now deserted him. They could not wait for material rewards later in life. They put material possessions ahead of fulfilling their destiny. In Philippians 3:18, he said of them, "*For many walk, of whom I have told you often, and now tell you even weeping, that they are the enemies of the cross of Christ: whose end is destruction, whose god is their belly, and whose glory is in their shame – who set their mind on earthly things.*"

To Timothy he wrote about Demas in 2 Timothy 4: 10, "*For Demas has forsaken me, having loved this present world, and has departed for Thessalonica.*"

Unfortunately, to focus on one's destiny to the end has been difficult for some people. Some have been distracted along the way. Like Gehazi, some people find it difficult to defer gratification for the cause of fulfilling destiny. However, with discipline and focus, we can fulfill our destiny.

Discouragement from within – not Joseph

We know that fulfilling one's destiny is a life-long journey. At certain points, the road may be winding, with bends and corners; the end-result may not be in view, but we must keep going. God chose Joseph from among his brethren, to protect and provide for them during a future time of famine. His journey to that time, where he was entrusted with the economy of Egypt, was not a straightforward one. He found himself the subject of envy and hatred from his brothers, so that they threw him into a pit without water. Then they sold him to the Midianites and he was bought in a slave market by Potiphar. In Potiphar's house, he had a time of reprieve as he settled into a regular job (although he was still missing his father's love and his hometown), when suddenly, in his fight for purity and integrity, he was thrown into jail and became a prisoner.

These events were tortuous enough to bring discouragement upon anyone. It was not clear to Joseph what God was doing with his life. He only knew that, as a young man, God had something great in store for him and that he was destined for a life of dominion and rulership. Throughout his youth he was God-fearing and maintained integrity and purity. This was revealed clearly in his reaction to Potiphar's wife when she tried to seduce him. Furthermore, his focus on God and desire to live a life of purity were confirmed by his response to Potiphar's wife. In Genesis 39:8-9 we read,

"But he refused and said to his master's wife, 'Look, my master does not know what is with me in the house, and he has committed all that he has to my hand. There is no one greater in this house than I, nor has he kept back anything from me but you, because *you are his wife. How then can I do this great wickedness, and sin against God?'"*

Joseph went from the pit to the slave market; then to Potiphar's house as a slave; and then to prison under suspicion of attempted rape. Through all these episodes, he maintained his worship of God, and never wanted to repay anyone with vengeance, nor sin against God. He never became discouraged, nor showed any trace of bitterness, even when the ungrateful butler completely forgot about him in jail. He kept on doing good until one day, because there arose a need of somebody prophetic to interpret a dream, the butler of Pharaoh remembered him.

Eventually, he was sent for, to appear before Pharaoh. This was the final stepping stone towards unfolding the dream he'd had when he was seventeen years old. He was now on the brink of dominion, rulership, influence and the manifestation of the authority that he had always carried within him. This was what he was destined for in life. It took him over thirteen years of suffering injustice, envy, hatred, lies, conspiracies and neglect. If this had happened to anyone else, I'm certain they would have grown bitter or been discouraged. They might have become so cynical that they believed God had forgotten them.

Discouragement, when our expectations are not realized, can make people turn away from the path of their destiny. Follow Joseph's example and refuse to harbor discouragement in your heart due to negative circumstances and setbacks.

Disobedience

One of the sweetest spiritual experiences we can enjoy in our lives is to listen to and obey the voice of the Lord. His instructions to us are in His written Word. In addition, the Lord speaks to us and instructs us through His Spirit. We can hear His voice speaking to us through His Spirit in us, or through other means. When we listen and obey His voice, and carry out His instructions, we are led into success and contentment. When we hear His instructions (either in His Word or through His Spirit) and refuse to carry them out, it grieves the Lord. Our disobedience robs us of enjoying the very best that God has for us.

When we persist in disobedience, we risk being shut out altogether from what God has planned for us. Anyone who wants to fulfill his or her destiny in God must be obedient to His Word and the leading of His Spirit. God will not let the disobedient child fulfill his or her destiny. We need to follow His leading and carry out all His instructions wholeheartedly. God speaking to us through David, the psalmist, said in Psalm 32:8-9:

"I will instruct you and teach you in the way you should go; I will guide you with My eye. Do not be like the horse or like the mule, which have no understanding, which must be harnessed with bit and bridle, else they will not come near you."

In other words, do not be hardened to the voice of the Holy Spirit or be stiff-necked like a mule.

Here is an example of someone who clearly heard the instructions of God but decided to be disobedient, stiff-necked and hard of hearing. In 1 Samuel 15:1-4 God spoke to Saul, the first king of Israel, through the prophet Samuel.

"The Lord sent me to anoint you king over His people, over Israel. Now therefore, heed the voice of the words of the Lord. Thus says the Lord of hosts: I will punish Amalek for what he did to Israel, how he ambushed him on the way when he came up from Egypt. Now go and attack Amalek, and utterly destroy all that they have, and do not spare them. But kill man and woman, infant and nursing child, ox and sheep, camel and donkey."

These were clear instructions from God to Saul. God wanted to use Saul, and the Children of Israel, to avenge what the Amalekites had done to earlier generations of Israel. So, Saul attacked the Amalekites and God helped him defeat them. But then in verse 9 we read,

"But Saul and the people spared Agag and the best of the sheep, the oxen, the fatlings, the lambs, and all that was good, and were unwilling to utterly destroy them. But everything despised and worthless, that they destroyed."

Disobedience to God can abort the fulfillment of our destiny. Saul chose to spare Agag and keep the best of the animals for himself. God was so grieved by this blatant act of disobedience, that He said to Samuel, *"I greatly regret that I have set up Saul as king, for he has turned back from following Me and has not performed My commandments."*

Because of Saul's persistent disobedience to God, he could not accomplish his destiny as the first king of Israel. In fact, in the very same chapter, Samuel the prophet spoke the Word of the Lord to him.

"For you have rejected the word of the Lord, and the Lord has rejected you from being king over Israel... The Lord has torn the kingdom of Israel from you today, and has given it to a neighbor of yours, who is better than you. And also the Strength of Israel will not lie nor relent. For, He is not a man that He should relent."

Thus, in the sight of the Lord, Saul's reign came to an end. Similarly, when we also persist in disobeying God, our destiny will be derailed, and we will not finish the course laid out for us.

Lack of submission to those placed in authority over us

Throughout our lifetime we are not the masters of our own affairs. As children we are nurtured by our parents and then, even when we become adults, the world's system ensures that we often have to work with somebody in authority over us. Some of those will have been placed there by God to guide us, provide us with the right opportunities, mentoring, correction and discipline that will enable us to become who God wants us to be in life. Problems arise though, when we do not respect those in authority or, worse still, when we disregard their authority or try to rebel against them.

King Saul's problems started when he got impatient with the prophet Samuel, who was his spiritual authority. Samuel had set a time to come to Saul and make a burnt offering for him before their battle with the Philistines. Samuel told him that he would arrive within seven days. The seventh day had not fully passed when Saul got impatient. In his eyes, Samuel was late in attending to him, the king. So, he asked for the burnt offering and peace offering and did the sacrifice himself, as if he were a priest.

Just as he had finished offering the sacrifice, Samuel appeared. He wasn't late as it was still within the seven days. The prophet asked Saul why he had done this. After his explanation, Samuel said to Saul,

"You have done foolishly. You have not kept the commandment of the Lord your God, which He commanded you. For now the Lord would have established your kingdom over Israel forever. But now your kingdom shall not continue. The Lord has sought for Himself a man after His own heart, and the Lord has commanded him to be commander over His people, because you have not kept what the Lord commanded you." (1 Samuel 13:13-14)

King Saul should have shown more respect and waited until the very end of the set time. Having a disregard for Samuel's spiritual authority was even more dangerous to him than his enemies, the Philistines.

Through Jonathan, his son, he won the battle. But he lost the kingdom.

It hadn't been long since Samuel had anointed Saul as king over Israel, but now Saul's respect for him had waned and he no longer valued Samuel's spiritual authority.

We see this in the Church today. A pastor's ministry may bring deliverance, promotion, elevation and prosperity into the lives of his congregation. But, after a while, they can become so familiar with him that they do not respect him or his word anymore. This is utter foolishness. His ministry and guidance could help fulfil their destinies and, without it, they will probably lose their way. Saul paid dearly for his lack of appreciation of the man of God.

In 2 Corinthians 10:8, Paul had to remind the Corinthian church again and again about the spiritual authority over them. He addressed those who are prone to always question someone's word or do something contrary, because they do not want anyone over them. Paul gently reminded them that the spiritual authority placed over them was primarily for their edification, not for their destruction. It was in their best interests to submit, so that it would go well for them in life. The opposite holds true too. Where you disregard the words of those in spiritual authority over you, your God-given destiny could crash off the rails and end up a burnt-out wreck.

Your destiny can be divinely fashioned by God, but by your wrong attitudes – particularly towards the men and women under whom God has placed you – you can be derailed and find yourself grappling with empty results. If Saul had continued taking his tutoring from the prophet Samuel, his reign as the first king of Israel could have been a successful one. He could have fulfilled his God–given destiny.

Perhaps, you may need to take a second look at those under whom God has placed you. Their spiritual authority over you is for your edification, not destruction. Learn to respect them.

Open rebellion

Open rebellion is an extreme destiny stopper. Those who are prone to rebel openly against authority do not last long in their journey. Open rebellion comes from pride which, God says in His word, He resists. With open rebellion you are setting yourself up against God. The classic case of rebellion in the Bible, in my opinion, is that of Korah, Dathan, Abiram and On (Numbers 16:1-3). They openly rose up against Moses' authority. They succeeded in persuading two hundred and fifty leaders of the whole nation of Israel to join them.

The nature of their rebellion was this: they said to Moses and Aaron, *"You take too much upon yourselves, for all the congregation is holy, every one of them, and the Lord is among them. Why then do you exalt yourselves above the assembly of the Lord?"*

This was not just a challenge to Moses' spiritual authority, it was an attempt to democratize the leadership. They all wanted a share and had no understanding of spiritual headship. Paul taught the Corinthians about headship in 1 Corinthian 11:3, saying, *"But I want you to know that the head of every man is Christ, the head of woman is man, and the head of Christ is God."* The head of that congregation of Israel was Moses. Moses was the head, not by the election of the people but by the appointment of God.

These men rose up against God's order. They wanted to be equal to Moses and Aaron in the decision-taking, in directing the assembly and in status. This is reminiscent of Lucifer's desire. He said to himself, *"I will ascend into heaven, I will exalt my throne above the stars of God; I will also sit on the mount of the congregation on the farthest sides of the north; I will ascend above the heights of the clouds, I will be like the Most High."* Lucifer did not want anyone to be above him. As an angel, a created being, he wanted to be on the same throne as the Most High.

Absurd as this was, what was really behind the open rebellion of Korah, Dathan, Abiram and On was this Lucifer-type desire to be on an equal footing with the head. What happened to them? They lost their lives immediately. In the most dramatic display of God's displeasure, the earth opened up and swallowed these men, their two hundred and fifty followers, their wives and children. They went, alive, down into a pit and the earth closed up over them.

There are a few foolhardy people around today like these men. People who simply cannot accept any headship over them for long. They do not submit to anyone. But be warned: this is a surefire way to run yourself into the pit and waste your God-given destiny.

Demonic stoppers and forces of darkness

Finally, there are direct forces of darkness, working through evil entities, demons and territorial spirits, that seek to stop people from achieving their God-given destinies.

Look at the case of the madman from the tomb in Gadarenes (Mark 5:1-18), mentioned earlier. After Jesus had delivered him from demonic bondage, he rightfully wanted to join Him and the disciples and go everywhere they went. This was because the people in the town had rejected the ministry of Jesus and asked Him to leave the area altogether. They were afraid of Him and His good works, especially when Jesus commanded the demons out of the man and into a herd of pigs who immediately threw themselves into the sea. To the locals, their livelihood was destroyed by the ministry of the Lord Jesus. Given the choice of having Jesus around or losing more economic assets, they chose to ask Jesus to leave town. Naturally, the freed man begged to go with them. But Jesus said to him, *"Go home to your friends, and tell them what great things the Lord has done for you, and how He has had compassion on you."*

In other words, the Lord Jesus implied that he had a destiny to fulfill in that region. He seemed to be telling him: "Your impact and influence is in this region, among your friends and those who know you. Go back to them and tell them the great freedom the Lord has given you." Mark 5:29 says, *"And he departed and began to proclaim in Decapolis all that Jesus had done for him; and all marveled."*

Then we read,

"Again, departing from the region of Tyre and Sidon, He came through the midst of the region of Decapolis to the Sea of Galilee. Then they brought to Him one who was deaf and had an impediment in his speech,

and they begged Him to put His hand on him. And He took him aside from the multitude, and put His fingers in his ears, and He spat and touched his tongue. Then, looking up to heaven, He sighed, and said to him, 'Ephphatha,' that is 'Be opened.' Immediately his ears were opened, and the impediment of his tongue was loosed, and he spoke plainly … And they were astonished beyond measure, saying, 'He has done all things well. He makes both the deaf to hear and the mute to speak.'" (Mark 7:31-37)

In Matthew's account of the second visit of Jesus to the Decapolis region (Matthew 15:30-31) we read,

"Then great multitudes came to Him, having with them the lame, blind, mute, maimed, and many others; and they laid them down at Jesus feet, and He healed them. So the multitude marveled when they saw the mute speaking, the maimed made whole, the lame walking, and the blind seeing; and they glorified the God of Israel."

The former madman had done a good job of spreading the word before Jesus returned. He testified to what God had done for him. He evangelized the whole area! By the time the Lord Jesus came a second time, the people were ready to receive Him. In fact, Mark recorded that they begged Him to put His hand on a mute person. Matthew's record was, *"Great multitudes came to Him having with them the lame, blind, mute, maimed, and many others and they laid them at His feet for Him to heal them."* This is the same Jesus whom, on His first visit, the townsfolk asked to leave.

The game-changer was the witness of the former madman. People believed him, seeing the dramatic change in his life. He affected the whole region and changed the spiritual atmosphere. By the time Jesus returned, the whole area flocked to Him. This time, the multitudes were glorifying God when Jesus ministered.

So, this man had a destiny all along. His destiny was to open the area for the Lord Jesus Christ and His ministry. He was called to change the spiritual climate in the region and make it receptive to the ministry of the Lord Jesus. A man with such a calling! Look at the way in which the devil had tried to lock up his destiny. He became demon possessed. A demon entered him and took over his life and when the Lord Jesus asked what its name was, the demon spoke through the man and said, "Legion." A Roman legion consisted of between two and six thousand foot soldiers. Presumably, around that number of demons were in the man. Because this man had a special destiny from God, the devil tried to mess up his life. Demons possessed him and turned him into a very violent person. He lived amongst the tombs, crying out and cutting himself with stones. The demons locked him up so that he was not free to fulfill his destiny.

When the Lord Jesus told the disciples that they were all sailing to the other side of the Sea of Galilee, look at what happened to them on the way. A strong storm arose against them. The Lord Jesus was coming to meet this man of Gadarenes and set him free, but a storm tried to stop them from coming. The storm was so severe that the disciples (and some of them had been professional fishermen) concluded that they were going to perish. Jesus was woken up and He rebuked the storm. This was an attempt by the regional or territorial demons to stop the destiny of this madman. They could sense that Jesus, coming into the area, would give this man his freedom, so they tried to prevent Him from coming.

The lesson is this: where demons and forces of darkness have locked up someone's destiny, by the authority and power of the name of Jesus, their destiny can be unlocked. Jesus set the man free and put him back on the road to his destiny. He told him, "Go home to your friends, and tell them what great things the Lord has done for you…". The man departed and began to proclaim his testimony in Decapolis. His evangelistic calling had been released by the Lord.

Today, we see people whose lives are bound by certain destructive behaviors and conduct. We see people locked in self-harm, unable to fulfill their destinies. Thanks be to God that we have a Savior who has come to set us free. By setting us free our destinies are also released. Some of us are called to have a huge impact, not only in one house, one church, one city or one location, but perhaps a whole region, a whole nation or even a whole continent! If territorial forces have been fighting you and have held you bound, if your destiny has been locked up in the hands of demonic forces, you can be set free! You can be released and commissioned to fulfill whatever the Lord has called you to do. The hold of territorial spirits can be broken in the name of the Lord Jesus Christ.

If you come from the type of background where no one you know has ever risen to do anything positive of real worth, do not despair. Jesus Christ, the Son of God, specializes in breaking bondage and releasing people from demonic destiny-stoppers.

When the Lord Jesus went to Zacchaeus' house and had lunch with him, Zacchaeus immediately had a transformation of heart and his conduct changed. The Lord Jesus declared, *"Today, salvation has come to this house, because he also is a son of Abraham for the Son of Man has come to seek and to save that which was lost."*

If Zacchaeus' salvation affected everyone in his house, think of the impact *your* salvation has on those around you. When Jesus visits, He breaks bondage, releases salvation and imparts destiny, all at the same time.

Conclusion: If You Are Derailed, Get Up!

Following one's destiny is a lifelong process. Some fall along the way, but others see the finishing line and run until they reach it.
In 2 Timothy 4:6-8 Paul clearly states,

"For I am already being poured out as a drink offering, and the time of my departure is at hand. I have fought the good fight, I have finished the race, I have kept the faith. Finally, there is laid up for me the crown of righteousness, which the Lord, the righteous judge, will give to me on that Day, and not to me only but also to all who have loved His appearing."

He could see the finishing line and he was confident that he had lived his life well. Despite starting so badly, persecuting Christians and destroying they very thing he was destined to build, he did not stay on the wrong road forever. The Lord Jesus appeared to him on the road to Damascus and revealed to him the purpose of his life. That was his divine encounter. The Lord told him He had appeared to him for this purpose: to make him a minister and a witness of the things he had seen and what He would reveal to him. Jesus told him He was sending him to the Gentiles to open their eyes, turn them from darkness to light, and from the power of Satan to God. Then, Paul began to know what he should live for and got on a new path of destiny instead of destroying the church. The Lord's appearance to him to turn him from the wrong road to the path of his destiny was sheer act of mercy and grace from God.

The grace of God fished him out of the ignorance of his destiny, turned him around and set him on the course of destiny. He never turned back from that course. If you also are ignorant of His appointed destiny for you at this point in time, He is ready to show you the same grace and mercy and reveal to you His purpose for your life. Secondly, lay hold of the principles that the aforementioned men and women of God laid hold of to fulfil their course. As Paul got back on track and began to live the life he was destined for, you can also get back on a new track for your destiny.

Likewise, David made many bad choices on the twisting pathway of his destiny. The most notable one was Bathsheba (2 Samuel 11). Not only did he get her pregnant when having an affair with her, he went so far down the wrong path that he did the unthinkable: he plotted to kill her husband, Uriah. And that wasn't all. Before that, he had married Michal because she was the daughter of the king. Then he married Ahinoam whilst a fugitive from Saul. He married Abigail because of her wisdom and sensibility. When he got into power, he added six other women. 2 Samuel 5:13 states that, *"And David took more concubines and wives from Jerusalem, after he had come from Hebron. Also more sons and daughters were born to David."*

The issue David had with Bathsheba did not just happen overnight. David, like Samson, seemed to have a problem with disciplining his sexual appetite. The Bathsheba incident was a disaster waiting to happen. Nevertheless, when confronted with his sin, David's heart broke. He was so crushed that he repented and threw himself upon the mercies of God.

At the end of his life, his testimony was this (Acts 13:36):

"For David, after he had served his own generation by the will of God, fell asleep, was buried with his fathers…"

In spite of everything, David repented and was restored to God and continued to live and fulfill his destiny. There has been no king in Israel like him.

You might have been distracted from your path, or may have done something foolish or disobedient. But, like Paul or David, you can get up and be restored to God's purposes and plan for your life.

Samson was eventually captured by the Philistines because of his affair with Delilah. Blinded, stuck in prison, his hair shorn, one would say that he had lost his destiny. He could not fulfill what God had planned for him to do in his life. He could not cross the finishing line, as Paul could say of himself. And the Philistines were singing with glee: *"Our god has delivered into our hands our enemy, the destroyer of our land, and the one who multiplied our dead"* (Judges 16:24).

But one day, when they were having a feast and their temple was full of men and women and lords, they sent for the blind Samson. They wanted Samson to be brought out for their entertainment. He was destined to be a deliverer and a judge of Israel, yet here he was, eyes taken out and made to be a jester in the court of the Philistines.

Samson was brought into their midst, but they did not realize that his hair had begun to grow. As his hair grew, his supernatural strength returned.

In the midst of such a large gathering of Philistines, knowing that his hair had grown again, Samson got up and prayed one last prayer in Judges 16:28-30: *"Then Samson called to the Lord, saying 'O Lord God, remember me, I pray! Strengthen me, I pray just this once, O God that I may with one blow take vengeance on the Philistines for my two eyes!' Samson took hold of the two middle pillars which supported the temple, and he braced himself against them, one on his right and the other on his left. Then Samson said, 'Let me die with the Philistines!' and he pushed with all his might and the temple fell on the lords and all the people who were in it. So the dead that he killed at his death were more than he had killed in his life.'*

At least at the time of his death he was still bringing deliverance to Israel from their enemies, the Philistines. However, it could have been a better story to tell if he had not asked to die with the Philistines. He could have prayed, "Let the Philistines die and let me live!" The Lord might have saved his life and given him a new opportunity to bring deliverance to Israel with his restored supernatural strength.

If your life is such that you feel you are not fulfilling your destiny, you can also get up from where you are now and turn back to God. Repent, call on His name, and He will restore His purposes and plans for your life. Samson, at the time of his death, killed in one moment more Philistines than he had done in the twenty years that he was judge of Israel.

You might have been tripped or derailed somewhere on your journey, but there is a comeback for you in God. The devil might think he has you in his grip, just as he had Samson in prison, but deep down in the miry clay you can sing like the prophet Micah. "*Do not rejoice over me, my enemy; when I fall, I will rise. When I sit in darkness, the Lord will be a light to me.*" (Micah 7:8)

Whatever state you find yourself in while reading this book, do not ever feel that your life is going nowhere and is of no value to society or your generation. As long as there is breath in your body, you can reconnect with God and ask to receive His grace and help, to know and fulfill your God-given destiny.

To those who have given up pursuing what they know to be their God-given destiny, remember that He will provide helpers to assist you. He has promised to lift you up over every obstacle and wall of resistance.

Everyone's life has a divine purpose. Everyone's life has divine potential. Let *your* life be remembered for the influence and impact you bring to others. Draw close to God and live in His wonderful will, then you will fulfill His destiny for your life and finish your race well.

About the Author

Rev. Wisdom Dafeamekpor is the Senior Pastor of Grace Chapel International in Accra Ghana. He also oversees several branches of the church in and outside Ghana.

He first trained as a chartered accountant, while an Assistant Pastor in Calvary Baptist Church in Accra, where he served between 1976 and 1991. In 1991, he started Grace Chapel International and devoted his time fully to the ministry.

His main ministry focus is that of a teacher of the Word and he has a heart for missions.

He is married to Lawrentia. They have been blessed with two sons (one of whom is the Youth Pastor) and a daughter.

Prayer to Become a Child of God

In Chapter 6, we talked about becoming a child of our Heavenly Father as the starting point of discovering our God-given destiny. If you have not yet received this sonship, or are not sure that you are a child of God, born again, saved for eternity, then I invite you to pray the following prayer to give your life to the Lord Jesus for His salvation.

First, believe that Jesus loves you and died for you. His death on the cross is the only price able to purchase for you eternal life. If you believe Jesus Christ died for you and are willing to give Him your life, confess this prayer from a sincere heart and you will become a child of God:

"Heavenly Father, I acknowledge that I am a sinner and have fallen short of standards. I deserve to be judged for eternity. But, I believe that you sent Jesus Christ, your only begotten Son into the world to die for me and bear my sins and judgment on the cross. I believe You raised Him from the dead on the third day and He is now seated at Your right hand as my Lord and Saviour.

Lord Jesus, I confess you as my Lord Saviour and King. Come into my life through Your Spirit and change me into a son (or daughter). From this day forward I will no longer live for myself, but for You. Thank You Lord; my life is now completely in your hands. Amen."

Prayer for Restoration of Your God-Given Destiny

Father, for those reading this book right now I pray that you will empower them, by your love and grace, that they may be catapulted into the destiny you have created them for. By your Spirit, open their eyes and their understanding, as you did for your servant Paul on the road to Damascus, that they may receive the knowledge of their destiny.

For those who began in your path and lost their way, I pray that you would restore them to the divine purpose and mission you planned for them. Let the help they need come to them now. For those whose strength and vision have been put out, I pray that you restore their strength and vision. In Jesus' name, I ask all this. Amen.